THE PHILOSOPHY
OF MATTER

THEORY IN THE NEW HUMANITIES

Series editor: Rosi Braidotti

Theory is back! The vitality of critical thinking in the world today is palpable, as is a spirit of insurgency that sustains it. Theoretical practice has exploded with renewed energy in media, society, the arts and the corporate world. New generations of critical 'studies' areas have grown alongside the classical radical epistemologies of the 1970s: gender, feminist, queer, race, postcolonial and subaltern studies, cultural studies, film, television and media studies.

This series aims to present cartographic accounts of emerging critical theories and to reflect the vitality and inspirational force of on-going theoretical debates.

Editorial board

Stacy Alaimo (University of Texas at Arlington, USA)

Simone Bignall (Flinders University, Australia)

Judith Butler (University of Berkeley, USA)

Christine Daigle (Brock University, Canada)

Rick Dolphijn (Utrecht University, The Netherlands)

Matthew Fuller (Goldsmiths, University of London, UK)

Engin Isin (Queen Mary University of London, UK, and University of London Institute in Paris, France)

Patricia MacCormack (Anglia Ruskin University, UK)

Achille Mbembe (University Witwatersrand, South Africa)

Henrietta Moore (University College London, UK)

Titles in the series so far

Posthuman Glossary, edited by Rosi Braidotti and Maria Hlavajova

Conflicting Humanities, edited by Rosi Braidotti and Paul Gilroy

General Ecology, edited by Erich Hörl with James Burton

Philosophical Posthumanism, Francesca Ferrando

THE PHILOSOPHY OF MATTER

A Meditation

RICK DOLPHIJN

BLOOMSBURY ACADEMIC

LONDON · NEW YORK · OXFORD · NEW DELHI · SYDNEY

BLOOMSBURY ACADEMIC
Bloomsbury Publishing Plc
50 Bedford Square, London, WC1B 3DP, UK
1385 Broadway, New York, NY 10018, USA
29 Earlsfort Terrace, Dublin 2, Ireland

BLOOMSBURY, BLOOMSBURY ACADEMIC and the Diana logo are
trademarks of Bloomsbury Publishing Plc

First published in Great Britain 2021

A catalogue record for this book is available from the British Library.

A catalog record for this book is available from the Library of Congress.

ISBN: HB: 978-1-3502-1189-6
         PB: 978-1-3502-1190-2
         ePDF: 978-1-3502-1191-9
         eBook: 978-1-3502-1192-6

Series: Theory in the New Humanities

Typeset by Integra Software Services Pvt. Ltd.
Printed and bound in Great Britain

To find out more about our authors and books visit www.bloomsbury.com
and sign up for our newsletters.

In memory of
Michel Serres (1930–2019),
mon ami …

CONTENTS

Acknowledgements   ix

Permissions   xii

PART ONE   Imagining the Undercurrent   2

I Don't Know Where This Is Going but I Know
Where to Begin…   5

The history of Cartesianism is the history of critique   11

Why our world demands a different form of thinking   15

Rewriting humanism   21

Imagination is what matters – it nurtures everything   25

PART TWO   This is not the Earth!   30

The philosopher is the geometer   33

The Deserted …   41

The pathologists of the earth   47

Become a target   53

PART THREE   I Can See Something   62

I am not a person, right?   65

Shadows in shadows   73

The cracks of the contemporary   79

The wound (I was born to embody)   91

PART FOUR Geometer, Show Me a New Earth   104

The geometer starts from a physics beyond critique   107

The geometers first axiom: A body is that which folds   121

The geometer maps that which is savage,
irregular, alive   133

The geometer maps how art objects   139

Earth – You are everywhere   147

References   152
Index   159

ACKNOWLEDGEMENTS

Contrary to popular belief, the art of writing a meditation does not lie in a striving for solitude. A meditation is a nomadology, an expedition during which one is fully depending on vital others, the human and non-human companions with whom I was fortunate enough to explore the new lands. We were nomads (as Karatani would put it) because our gifts were real (not reciprocal), because the land we travelled was unlimited and we had to move together, as a pack. The festivals, the exhibitions, the cultural events, the conferences, lectures and research stays introduced me to lives and happenings unimaginable before, dear memories that have stayed with me when I retreated in the Netherlands, or in Hong Kong, where I also spend a substantial part of the year.

Of course, I want to thank 'all that mattered' for moving me/the world around me in a good way. A few names, though, that need to be mentioned: I want to thank my colleagues at Utrecht University: Eugène van Erven, Liesbeth Groot Nibbelink, Sigrid Merx, Iris van der Tuin, Nanna Verhoeff, Berteke Waaldijk and above all Rosi Braidotti, for her comradeship and for teaching me academic responsibility. I want to thank the University of Hong Kong for the long-term Honorary Professorship (2017–23) and my colleagues there: Ian Holliday, Nicole Huang, Gina Marchetti, Winnie Yee and above all Gray Kochhar-Lindgren, for all the wonderful projects we ran together and for being the best teacher I know. Thanks also to the

Common Core Staff and the Department of Comparative Literature. Also a big thanks to Anna Maria Guasch, Christian Alonso and the Art, Globalisation and Interculturality Research Group at the University of Barcelona for offering me a Visiting Professorship (2019–20).

Thanks to my students and colleagues at Media and Culture Studies (and in particular within Arts and Society), the Humanities Honours Program, the HKU-UU exchange program. Thank you (in no particular order): Stacy Alaimo, Pau Alinsa, Karen Barad, Joff Bradley, Andreas Broeckmann (and V2_), Gustav Broms, Levi Paul Bryant, Ian Buchanan, Arthur Bueno, Maren Butte, Jason Coe, Mark Coeckelbergh, Felicity Colman, Christine Daigle, Camilla Eeg-Tverbakk, Thomas Eller (and Taoxichuan), Silvia Fehrmann, Isis Germano, Rutger de Groot, Donna Haraway, Bernd Herzogenrath, Daniel Ho (and Tai Kwun), Isaac Leung (and Videotage), Janina Loh, Birgit Kaiser, Woosung Kang, Jon Kessler, David Kew, Katie King, Jae-Yin Kim, Tove Kjellmark, Jussi Koitela (and Frame), Katerina Kolozova, Bogna Konior, Kristiina Koskentola, Bose Krishnamachari, Alex Taek-Gwang Lee, Andrea Leine, Wessie Ling, Patricia McCormack, Stuart McLean, Yates Norton (and Rupert Contemporary Art), Timothy O'Leary, Daan F. Oostveen, Adrian Parr, Tim Persent, Bryan Reynolds, David Roden, Stanimir Panayotov, Sverre Raffnsøe, Harijono Roebana, Martin Rosenberg, Arun Saldanha, Tony See, Tim Simpson, Lars Spuybroek, Mads Rosendahl Thomsen, Toshiya Ueno, Lucas van der Velden (and Sonic Acts), Willem van Weelden, Heather Ware, Agnieszka Wolodzko, Jo Wei, Nathan Widder, Xiao Yu and Rob Zwijnenberg.

Thanks to Tsz Man Chan for the Papay Gyro Nights, for your creativity and for everything else; to Nick Polson for all the help; to the immensely talented Oscar Yik Long Chan for his beautiful drawings; and to Trixie Tsang for being brilliant and amazing. Thanks to my editor, Liza Thompson, and the anonymous reviewers at Bloomsbury. A final thanks to the people of Hong Kong for showing me and the rest of the world how to live one's wounds beautifully.

Between Rotterdam and Hong Kong 2019/2020

Rick Dolphijn

PERMISSIONS

I am not a quick thinker. Some thoughts stick with me for a decade before they start or stop making sense (again). For this meditation, I worked with some ideas that were published elsewhere, in a different form. Sometimes the ideas are hardly recognizable, sometimes the claim I make has changed 180 degrees. Nevertheless, parts or fragments printed here, can be traced to an earlier source and that is why, to exclude any conflict in interest, I want to thank the publishers involved generously for their cooperation.

Part 2
Contains fragments of
Dolphijn, R. 2012. Undercurrents and the Desert(ed): Negarestani, Tournier and Deleuze map the poly-tics of a 'New Earth'. In: *Postcolonial Literatures and Deleuze: Colonial Pasts, Differential Futures*. B. M. Kaiser and L. Burns (ed.). London: Palgrave Macmillan. 199–216

Part 3
Contains fragments of
Dolphijn, R. 2011. 'The World of the Grotesque is the Darkness within Us': The Noir Geoaesthetics of Murakami's Nakata. in: *Fast Capitalism* 8:1

Part 4
Contains fragments of
Dolphijn, R. 2014. The Intense Exterior. In: *Performance Studies: Key Words, Concepts, and Theories*. Bryan Reynolds (ed.). London: Palgrave Macmillan.
Dolphijn, R. 2016. Critical Naturalism: A Quantum Mechanical Ethics. In: *Rhizomes: Cultural Studies in Emerging Knowledge. Special Issue Quantum Possibilities, the Work of Karen Barad*. Edited by Karin Sellberg and Peta Hinton. Issue 30

Part 1

IMAGINING THE UNDERCURRENT

In sharp contrast with the idea that philosophy's concern is rational thought (the *cogito* according to Descartes) and proceeds through critique (according to Kant), the first part of this meditation explores how the contemporary *matters* and how it can be *imagined otherwise*. I therefore need to distance myself first from the History of Philosophy (with capitals) as it *prevents* me from experiencing everything that happens 'with the times', everything the Earth is able to reveal. I search for a wild and untamed thinking that cannot be included in the political, religious or economic streams of what I call 'the present'. I search for the part of philosophy that has systematically been marginalized by the History of Philosophy, but that also cannot be 'included in it', or, refuses to be included in it. I search for a stubborn, immanent, naturalist thinking that was always ready to restore a belief in the Earth and in life in all of its human and non-human realizations...

Starting from imagination, a theme I take from Benedictus de Spinoza, thinking the 'undercurrent', as I call it, is desperately needed if we search for a philosophy able to undermine the powers of 'the present'. Spinozist materialism is and *always has been* the creative act that shows us how to live our lives otherwise.

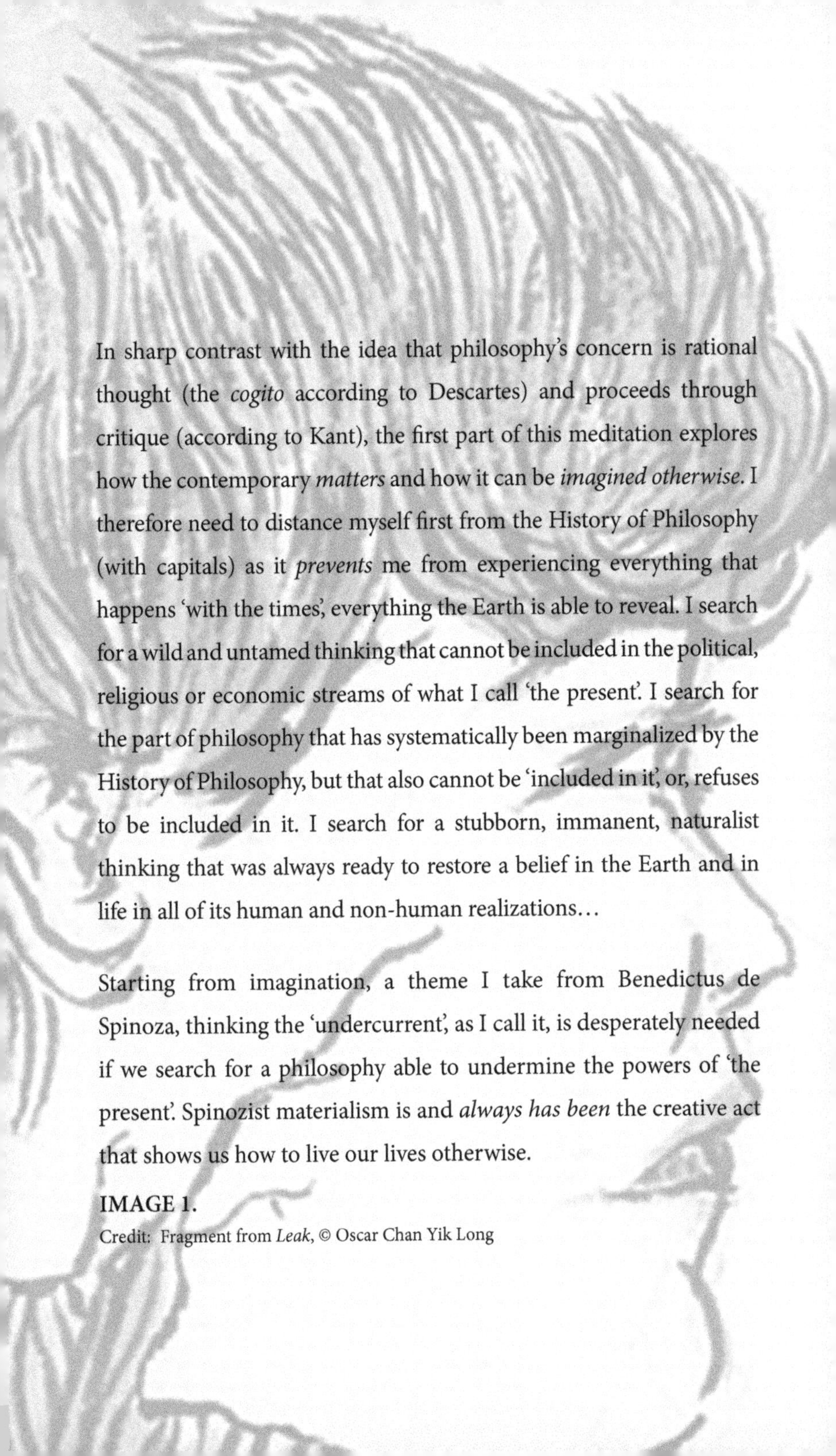

IMAGE 1.
Credit: Fragment from *Leak*, © Oscar Chan Yik Long

I Don't Know Where This Is Going but I Know Where to Begin…

Benedictus de Spinoza is one of those rare thinkers capable not only of inventing thought-provoking concepts but also of immediately confronting us with a fully other way of perceiving, of offering us a wholly other earth. An earth much more beautiful than the earth dominating our fantasies for so long, much more vibrant and hopeful: *an earth more earthly*. Spinoza's philosophy was fully realized in the year 1677, when, right after his early death, his friends were bold enough to publish his *Ethica: Ordine Geometrico Demonstrata* together with the many other writings Spinoza himself (rightfully) did not dare to publish during his lifetime. His ideas were too radical for the Theologians, the Cartesians and the Regents (in particular the Oligarchs/the 'Orangists', followers of the family Van Oranje, which still reigns the Netherlands) of his time. Or to phrase it differently: within the *religious, humanist and capitalist* realities that dominated his day and age, there is no room for Spinozism. The dark and connective nature of Spinozism as opposed to light and selective Cartesianism (humanism) was considered a danger to the established order. Antonio Negri (1970) is right when he considers Descartes's *Discourse* the bildungsroman of the bourgeois. Its appeal to the powerful is *the only reason* Cartesianism became the dominant structure for thought until today.

Spinoza's work definitely would not qualify for that. This was not a problem of his day and age. On the contrary, Spinozism will never be in line with the dominant powers that be. The reason for this fundamental rejection is, in essence, relatively simple: Spinozism is a kind of thinking that does not function with 'the present', as I would like to call it. The three abovementioned forces (the religious, humanist and capitalist realities), in turn, jostle one another for domination of the everyday life. Spinozism cannot play 'a part' in this; it is necessarily a *revolutionary* power that might not be present, but that is definitely there. Spinozism can 'happen' all the time; its immense powers are creeping out anywhere. I will refer to them in this part as 'the Spinozist undercurrent', sometimes simply 'the undercurrent'.

The Spinozist undercurrent was generously released with the publication of the *Ethics*, but it was announced and at work long before this particular era. Perhaps from the sixth century BC, when all over the world this new form of thinking celebrated some 'momentum' (with thinkers like Jeremiah, Lao Tzi, Heraclites, Pythagoras and perhaps Sittarda Gaotama). I am sure that there are many more, less canonized, pagan, nomadic, marginal thinkers who enriched their contemporaries in a similar way. Karatani ([2012] 2017) is right when he signals that the connections that made up this particular momentum (around the sixth century BC) were *not* based on political, religious or economic bonds. The momentum was spun between all sorts of free spirits that were, in a way, searching for ways to *map a naturalism and an ethics*, like Spinoza. When looking at the origins of philosophy, Spinoza himself (see 1995; Letter 56 §11) also sees how his ideas resonate in the works of Democritus, Archimedes, Zeno, Epicurus and Lucretius. Therefore, although we can find momentums, or some other form of fulcrum in the history of thought, it is good to remind ourselves immediately that undercurrents are never contained by space or time. Undercurrents flow in many unforeseen directions and can always surface. They can always begin freeing the free spirits.

Why do I refer to this as the *Spinozist* undercurrent? Because in my mapping of the history of thought, Spinoza's naturalist Ethics offers us the most elaborate, rigid, deep and earthy analysis of what the undercurrent is about. Next to that, although fiercely rejected by those in power, the publication of *The Ethics* accelerated this wholly other way of perceiving, which surfaced again in the works of Friedrich Nietzsche and Gilles Deleuze; with writers like George Eliot (Spinoza's first translator in English), Marcel Proust and Virginia Woolf; with performance artists like Antonin Artaud; with mathematicians like Gottlieb Leibniz, Henri Bergson and Albert Einstein; with biologists like Jakob von Uëxkull; and with psychologists like William James and Gilbert Simondon. Even today, 350 years after the appearance of Spinoza's writings, from cultural theory (Rosi Braidotti) to neuroscience (Antonio Damasio) to science studies (Isabelle Stengers), but even more so with increasing interest in performance art, installation art and bio art that really marks the start of the twenty-first century with such figures as Patricia Piccinini,

Adam Zaretsky and Nathalie Jeremijenko. Equipped with *the same raw affirmative power*, the Spinozist undercurrent causes revolutions in thought, installing an activism and an urgency that sets every field of knowledge in movement.

I already noted that the undercurrent in thought that asks for our attention cannot be *present*. It refuses to be formed (moulded) and can be recognized only by the fact that it causes free spirits. Throughout history, this undercurrent has opened up many traditions in thought and has mattered everywhere. My meditation is strongly entangled with the ideas of Spinoza, Gilles Deleuze and Michel Serres, as they, for me, echo the thoughts of my new materialist, posthumanist and eco-feminist allies best. Also, they are, *to a similar extent*, fabricated with the arts – by the dancers, the performance artists, the architects and the writers that accompany me. Imagining a philosophy of matter, with my companions from theory, my thoughts have to be intervened constantly by the arts. Parasitical as both philosophy and the arts need to be (and very often on each other), I should, therefore, parallel to the propositions, definitions and scholia of Spinoza, mention the importance of the figures given rise to in the work of the writer Haruki Murakami.

The figures of Murakami (Nakata, Marie Akigawa, Aomame, Kafka, Colonel Sanders and many others) come into existence *solely* in their travels; their nomadic trajectories *give rise to concepts* that force us to think about the realities of today, cracking them open and allowing the cold wind from the outside, the rain, the fantastic and the unforeseen to enter the scene. Writing between the many Japanese traditions that are aimed at proposing to us the 'disconcerting picture of the human predicament', the art scene of post-atomic Japan, in my view, is best capable of mapping what matters in the contemporary. Especially the works of Murakami – as they, in turn, echo the films of Francois Truffaut, the music of Ellington, Mozart and Lennon & McCartney – are unprecedented in proving that the so-called 'fictional' figures produced capture the matters of the contemporary best.

But I must begin with Spinoza. The way of perceiving that Spinozism proposes always makes the first intervention into the realities of the present. Spinozism is what happens *with the times and together with* the present; it makes up what I call 'the contemporary': to map and to situate the intensities it co-creates, the temporal and eternal 'forces' it makes possible. To realize that, I will hardly contemplate on 'particular cases' of the religious, humanist and capitalist realities of the day. Rather, I begin from the cracks that break open the present, that allow for all sorts of wild and untamed forms of *unforeseenness*: What different lives are these cracks giving rise to? Lives that have no history and future, that function neither through identity nor through difference. Lives that are earthly, unthought-of, that are immanent, relational, in-movement and un-human. Lives that are in every way revolutionary. Remembering the fields of knowledge in which Spinozism manifests itself in the contemporary, one might even wonder whether there is any other type of revolution possible other than the Spinozist (capable of breaking open the powers of the present).

The history of Cartesianism is the history of critique

To understand how Spinoza initiates his critique of Descartes, we should begin by noting that for Spinoza the world does not start from fixed entities; there 'is' no subject, just as there 'is' no object. More formally, for Spinoza, the external world (the Great Outside) exists *only* in how it *affects* the body, while the body exists *only* in how it *is affected by* the external world. Through our predator binocular vision (and the 'edging' through which it sharpens the folds), our poor nose, our stiff neck and our skilful hands, we give form to our bodies as we give form to our outside; we imagine objects and trust our appetite. We imagine the (same?) snowflake everywhere; we imagine the (same?) Other everywhere. Captured in their laboratory, the physicists imagine light to be a particle… or a wave… or both, at the same time. Only through the bodily affections can we produce a thought, whereas the body itself can only be known in how it is affected by external bodies (see, for instance, E2P19). This means that the idea 'of' the body is consequential to its own situational and relational existence (and the other way around). Thus, Spinoza offers us an *absolute* relativity (the body and the mind, but also the subject and the object, the inside and the outside, are consequential to each other), as opposed to the *relative* relativity of Descartes (*everything starts with the human mind, the *cogito*, the 'I think').

Since *only relations actually exist*, one wonders what keeps 'this life' in movement. When defining the individual, Spinoza first notes that individual things are finite and have a determinate existence; in other words, they function as one (see 2D7). Yet he adds something to this, which is of the greatest importance: that any individual necessarily consists of a series of individuals, ad infinitum. Thus, instead of taking the individual as a point of departure (albeit the organic unity (as with Rélay) or even 'a thing' or 'an object', which I will come back to later in this book), Spinoza claims that the individual (or more accurately, any possible individuality) is both immanent and creative. It is immanent because there is no 'rule' that tells us what the individual looks like beforehand. This means that for Spinoza, there is no 'organism', no genus or species, and to translate this into post-68 theory, there is no sex, colour, class or age from which to start (and thus no sex, colour, class, age etc. from which to liberate). Consequently, there are also no fixed relationships between particular individuals; what is, in one situation, food for the one is poison for the other, or the other way around. Again, this is an absolute relativism: *all is relations within relations.*

Spinoza's individual is 'that which is united in one action' or 'that which functions as one' (again see, for instance, E2D7) and changes its reality (actively and passively) according to the way these relations change (i.e. it is not dependent upon particular 'things'). Building upon this reality of change, Spinoza says the *essence* of any individual becoming is based on the idea that this individual will always intend to persevere in its being (in any possible dimensionality). Essence should be read in its classical use, as the (non-existent) present particle of 'esse' (to be, making 'essens'), as also proposed by Cicero (according to Seneca). It conceptualizes how any individual not only comes to be according to the reality of change but also, at the same time, that it searches for ways to actually live this reality of change. In tune with what we today call the Second Law of Thermodynamics (which articulates entropy and promises the deterioration of any existing system), any individual (a force) is thus forced, for the sake of its own survival (we trust), to anticipate upon new modes of existence within the reality of constant change.

So, what 'is' this individual in Spinozist thought? First, we must keep in mind that for Spinoza, the individual *can be anything* that functions as one and that aims at persevering in its being. This can be a human being, but also a group of human beings. It can be a cloud, an island, an interface or an ecosystem. It can also be what we provisionally call the bond between the animal and the plant (the wasp and the orchid), the sympathy between the cloud and the human or, with a reference to Bateson (2002, 317), the 'system' that comes into being in the event of felling a tree: the system between 'tree-eyes-brain-muscles-axe-stroke-tree', the material assemblage that accompanies the felling. For this system also functions as one and, as Bateson (idem) repeatedly emphasizes, *thinks* from its oneness (the set of transformations that function with one another). Contemporary developments in neurophysiology – especially when analysed purely mathematically and not accepting the dominant prejudice of (Cartesian) neuroscience that thinking happens only in the brain – similarly push its focus towards the transformation processes. Not surprisingly.

It is not easy to let go of a system of thought that somehow played such an important role in the History of Philosophy, but comparing the refined and elegant ecology of Spinoza to the blunt anthropocentrism of Descartes, one wonders whether anyone *ever* truly believed Descartes.

Why our world demands a different form of thinking

Stripping the world from its Cartesian dreams, the acute attention to the processes of transformation that Spinoza reveals to us is what Michel Serres shows us best in our times. Having grown up alongside the riverbeds of the Garonne, Serres has to see the Garonne not simply as a river that flows but much more as an inevitable companion, a sister, a mother, a friend that is not far away from Vincennes, where he lived during the later part of his life. The Garonne river was always flowing within him, within his body, within his thoughts. Inevitably. The Garonne was active in all of his ideas, and at the same time, all of his ideas have the Garonne as their object (necessarily). Therefore, he concludes: 'When I think, I become what I am thinking' (Serres 2015, 21, my translation). Murakami puts it differently, yet the same. In a short story called *an Independent Organ*, doctor Tokai asks us many questions but makes us think about only one thing in the end: '*What* in the world, am I?' (2018, 144, my emphasis).

The ideas that the system generates rise from its united body, from the oneness established and have its body as its object. It is for this reason that I call Spinoza and the Spinozist undercurrent the revolution that is necessarily materialist. I use 'materialist' here with its double meaning: starting from a non-Cartesian geometry – there is no point of departure called a 'Subject' and no position relative to it called an 'Object' – and from immanence, translated as an interest in matter and what matters and not differentiating between the two. Matter (the noun) and to matter (the verb) are, in the end, the same thing.

I want to maintain the radical difference between the two forms of thought in our times (the Cartesian critical perspective and Spinozist materialism), although it must be noted that it is very difficult not to make mistakes in this. What seems Spinozist at first may prove deeply Cartesian when given a more thorough analysis, and, of course, the converse happens just as often. In popular science books today, for instance, a certain form of Spinozism seems to be at work in how biologists look at how plant theory reconceptualizes 'thinking'. Scholars like Daniel Chamovitz claim not only that plants are sentient (which we can already read in Darwin) but also that 'plants know' (Chamovitz 2012, 137). Not starting from the brain, from 'consciousness' or 'knowledge', Chamovitz seems to start from affect, from how plants respond to the aromas that surround them, from how they respond to being touched and are aware of gravity and of their 'own past'. But in order for Chamovitz's ideas to not fall back into an implicit Cartesian idea of subjectivity here, thinking should not to be situated 'in' the plant.

What thinks is the transformation between 'its' colour and 'its' form ('it' is thus not referring back to the plant but to the whole material assemblage that functions as the object for this idea: nature). And what thinks, to give another example, is also between the sun and its leaves. More interesting, in that sense, is how anthropologists such as Eduardo Kohn show us how forests think. Analysing how the forests around Ávila (in Amazonian Ecuador) are animate, stressing that these forests house an 'emergent loci of meanings' (2013, 72), Kohn aptly practices the Spinozist geometry of immanence, combining ancient animist ideas of spirituality with contemporary 'postorganic' neurophysiology. It shows the reality of what Brian Massumi (2014, 31) calls 'creative bodying' and its animatedness as 'lived'.

What Kohn hints at is precisely what Rosi Braidotti (2019) keeps stressing: that 'indigenous knowledges' and the alternatives it offers to Cartesian anthropocentrism should not be seen as our past; *they are our future.* Our only possible future, I would like to add.

Undercurrents travel in many unexpected directionalities and dimensionalities. When contemporary quantum mechanics (as opposed to nineteenth-century electromechanics) claims that correlations have a physical reality and that to which they correlate does not, as Karen Barad (2007a) shows us, this resonates with Spinozism as it somehow resonates with contemporary bioart, epigenetics and environmental activism (to name just a few of the terrains where this is happening). Showing how semiochemicals and visual signs compose new bodies, create new alliances (a reproductive system that concerns a wasp and an orchid, for instance) is also in line with this strand in materialist philosophy. And when paleobiologists (e.g. Simon Conway Morris (2003)) study the convergences between lakes, fishes, stones and weeds, but also wind and temperature, showing how similar eco-spheres, in different geographical locations, give rise to similar organic life forms (which are, interestingly enough, not genetically related), do they not also show us that Cartesian/Modern thinking, in all of its appearances, is a fraud?

Chamovitz and Kohn and many other thinkers and artists both within and outside of academia are doing fascinating work with respect to questioning the Cartesianism/Modernism that is so deeply embedded in us. Nevertheless, when it comes to reconceptualizing thought and the idea of thinking, Spinoza himself is still the most revolutionary of all thinkers. In his letter to Schaller, dated October 1674 (Letter LXII (LVII)), he claims that a stone too, while in movement, must be capable of some form of thinking and knowing. The stone, too, is responsive to its environment, undergoes transformations because of it and does whatever lies in its power to persevere in its being!

The conclusion is that freeing ourselves from Cartesian dualism means practicing the idea that 'the order and connection of ideas is the same as the order and connection of things' (2p7). We must understand that 'words are bodily movements', as contemporary Spinozist Pierre-François Moreau (1994, 310, my translation) concluded, just as the life of democracy concerns a material organization. All good ideas in a particular era produce new layers upon the earth, new strata upon which a new form of life may develop. All bodies and their ideas always follow from a very 'unforeseen' series of materials that are not so much bound together because of their unity in substance (because we label them 'organic') but because they 'share a childhood', as I would like to phrase it. Actively or passively, they have been functioning together; their relation mattered, and somehow, it is according to this relation (only!) that they survive. Thus, although 'we have never been modern' – as Bruno Latour assures us, stressing that modern dualisms were based on wrong (Cartesian) assumptions about the world (*incertain et inutile*, as Pascal already put it) – all of these dualisms have been *real in their consequences* (and continue to be realized). The mass extinctions, the plastiglomerate that promises to be the new top layer of our earth, the large increase in atmospheric CO_2 ... *all of the crises of today* show us the perverse reality of modernism.

'There was a strange stillness', Rachel Carson ([1962] 2000, 22) wrote in her prophetic book *Silent Spring*. Carson foresaw that we became blind to the fact that '[t]he history of life on earth has been a history of interaction between living things and their surroundings' (idem, 23). As we are blinded by the increase of profit as our sole objective, our croplands have been silenced because of single-crop farming (which is maintained only through the extensive use of insecticides or 'biocides', as she calls them). Then, it did not take long before also our pastures, in fear of infection (mad cow disease, swine fever, birds pest, indeed... Covid-19), were cleared, as we are locking up 40 per cent of all mammals on earth in barns for our own consumption (on a diet of steroids). Now, in the year 2021, we are clearing our cities from ourselves, in fear of viruses. This is the paradox of our time: we have never been modern, yet we must search for a new way to live in the Ruins of Modernism, which are everywhere.

Of course, it may very well be that we will not succeed...

Rewriting humanism

Perhaps Kohn's writings on forests, combined with the Garonne river in Michel Serres, show us most convincingly how we are immersed in animated landscapes, how animated landscapes are immersed in us and how this relation causes thoughts and ideas to appear within this immanent individuality that is both inside and outside of us. It shows us how the immanent bodies and their ideas of the contemporary cannot and should not be divided into organic or inorganic, natural or technical, or indeed, any of the oppositions according to which Cartesianism organizes the earth. It shows us the impossibility of a Humanism that starts from a 'human' perspective and not from the relations. It is time we realised (echoing Latour) that we have always been 'before or after' Humanity; we have never even 'been' Human.

Let me phrase this in a proper materialist fashion: no one was ever human by birth, but shared a childhood with all that was assembled upon the surfaces of our life. Refusing to accept 'Man' as its point of departure, Spinozist materialism cannot but conclude that all bodies persisting in being are necessarily good in themselves and search to strengthen their particular idea of goodness by creating new alliances, new resonances with bodies that are good to them, that increase their power to act, that aim to exist only from the necessity of their own nature and are determined to act by themselves alone.

Spinozist materialism, revived since 1968, started with strong advocacy for those fellow humans that did not fit our definition of 'man', bringing to our attention those for whom humanism had failed, demanding us to rethink the female, the black, the aged and the sexed, but also the sick, the wounded and the traumatized. More recently, but still inspired by 1968, materialism turned to the animal, the natural and the non-organic bodies. However, it is important to note that this materialist rethinking, if done well, is done not so much in relation to the dominant forms of power (contrary to critical thinking, or Cartesianism). It cannot restrict itself to responding to Cartesianism, because then, once again, it would restrict itself to being only a philosophy of liberation, a relative change. As stressed before, Spinozist materialism has always already lived as a nomadic and inclusive entity in itself, actualizing wholly other landscapes, wholly other forms of life about which we were previously unaware. Braidotti (2019) is right: Spinozist materialism asks us to always write *beyond the human condition* – a true philosophy of freedom for all, human and non-human. Thus, in the end, this materialism is not so much a task, solely, for 'the marginal groups' of society; it concerns everything, everywhere. Or better, it concerns all realizations of us/ in us/with us.

Let us call this a geophilosophy.

It is time to understand the unprecedented power of materialism, this burst of creativity that proceeds in geophilosophy and that materializes in the arts, as well as the joy and freedom it has to offer to all individualities. Let me therefore come back to Serres's claim posed above: 'When I think, I become what I am thinking' (Serres 2015, 21, my translation), the motto of the geophilosopher who has nothing less than the entire earth as its virtual body. With a body that is soft, that is transformative, that is ghostly, perhaps, the geophilosopher has the power to traverse all that matters. The geophilosopher offers us an idea of thinking that perhaps comes closest to a contemporary version of what was once called 'metempsychosis', by the Pythagoreans in antiquity. Metempsychosis can best be summarized by the following phrase from Empedocles: 'I was in other times a boy and a girl, a bush and a bird, a silent fish in the sea...' (quoted in Simondon [2004]2011, 22, note 2). Particularly in its modern (nineteenth-century) readings, which implicitly accept chronology as the one and only nature of time, metempsychosis is associated with reincarnation (and with non-modern forms of thought, such as Buddhism and Hinduism).

But there is absolutely no reason to ridicule metempsychosis on the basis of modernity's preference for linear time. Even more so, metempsychosis has nothing to do with the modernist idea that the human mind equals the human brain and that human thought should be considered 'the starting point for knowledge and the paradigm for knowledge' (Gaukroger 1989, 50), which is how metempsychosis is discussed in the writings of Proust, Melville, Pynchon and Joyce. Let us rather follow Borges, who saw that the bullet that killed J.F.K. was an old one:

> It was the silken cord given to viziers in the East, the rifles and bayonets that cut down the defenders of Alamo, the triangular blade that slit a queen's throat, the wood of the Cross and the dark

nails that pierced the flesh of the Redeemer, the poison kept by the Carthaginian chief in an iron ring on his finger, the serene goblet that Socrates drank down one evening.

(Borges [1989] 1998, 326)

What thinks, what acts, what does is embodied, but embodied in change. It can be a bush and a bird, a silken cord and a cross.

Consequently, there is nothing 'human' or even organic about metempsychosis. A soul, an idea, a *conatus* (the term Spinoza uses for something like 'instinct', through which, for instance, 'the stone thinks', as discussed above) *must* transform in order to secure its own survival. And in doing so, it is not restricted by our humanist taxonomies (why could not the lethal bullet turn into the lethal staircase? (idem, 116)). In his introductory course on general psychology, Gilbert Simondon ([2004] 2011) already suggests this revitalization, this fully transformative definition of all souls, adding to it (and making sure) that after modernity (after Cartesian Humanism, after critical thinking), it is the immanent mapping of sameness (relations, resonances) that marks contemporary metempsychosis. The search for sameness (for relations, for new resonances) forces all souls to travel continuously, reinventing themselves through that which matters, becoming with the bush or with the triangular blade, creating new alliances and new ideas.

Imagination is what matters – it nurtures everything

The I is the boy and the girl, the bush and the bird while it is a silent fish in the sea, because in living this matter, in being involved, the boy, the girl, the bush, the bird and the silent fish in the sea have become its object of thinking (and thus they gave rise to its idea). That is the materialism of Spinoza's physics and metaphysics, panphysics and transphysics. It moves through desire or appetite and introduces us to what Spinoza calls the first kind of knowledge. When reading Spinoza, the first kind of knowledge is understood as (opinion and) imagination. In Spinozist commentary, the second kind of knowledge (rational knowledge) and the third kind of knowledge (divine or eternal knowledge or, interestingly enough, 'intuitive science') receive the most attention. Yet already in the 1960s de Deugd (1966) stressed that the power of the first kind of knowledge is a great deal more important than often believed.

Imagination is strongly connected to appetite, the never-ending hunger that drives all possible and impossible bodies and that is of vital importance to the perseverance of the world that we live in. Appetite is a raw force that is often in all kinds of conflict with the religious, humanist and capitalist currents of the day it. *Erst kommt das fressen, dan kommt die moral*, as Bertolt Brecht (1928) said it. Raw appetite both feeds and poisons the imagination. But only this way we may see the island behind the island, the earth underneath the earth, the new forms and alliances that we had been blind to. Imagination, therefore, gives us the raw, untamed, unforeseen confrontations that make up the everyday, that give form to our bodies and our thoughts, our events and our ideas differently, as they are 'creative' in the most elementary sense of the word.

The imagination, the first kind of knowledge, has the body as its moral requirement, since it perishes after the body dismembers (after life ends) (see E5p40). It injects us with the most materialist, the most creative and definitely the maddest and most impossible ideas. Imagination, out of naivety, playfulness and simply out of necessity (the need to find a way to survive), is able to give rise to new surfaces and vitalize new environments that smoothen and deterritorialize the earth. Imagination welcomes us to one million infinity rooms (as Yayoi Kosama calls them) that are eager to give you a life, however brief and un/real! The neurotic, the psychotic, the fantastic bodies, frantically in search for ways to survive, relate to an earth the Others could never see. Wild and restless and above all dangerous, imagination gives rise to a singular life, struggling with its appetites, unwilling (and unable) to take control. Yet in experimenting with the body, always already forming new connections, new convergences are at work within new alliances (new bodies), new ideas come about and new thoughts emerge that are products of this alliance.

Spinoza keeps warning us for the dreadful mistakes that imagination makes, for the strange things it makes us see. Imagination actualizes Cthulu and Baal. Imagination gave us racial traits, race in general. All forms of patriarchy, the idea that we have to put nature on a wreck, the idea that winning oil (bitumen) from sands is actually smart, all of this comes down to the first kind of knowledge. More devastating even: imagination installed dualisms into our world *and made us act accordingly*. Spinoza is right: it is not our body but our imagination that imprisons us. Imagination has the power to materialize a set of morals in such a way that it organizes the modern world, producing the religious, humanist and capitalist reality itself. All the strategies of domestication and systems employed by it stem from our imagination. Imagination has the power to lock us all up in a firm system of dogmas and beliefs which are extremely difficult to resist. It is because of imagination that Christ is everywhere, present in every part of our daily life.

Appetite always confronts us with other matters, offers us new thoughts, questions the present in innumerable ways. Or, as we will soon find out: there is always another earth! Lucretius, in his *De Rerum Natura*, probably written around 50 BC, concluded 'the earth is not something alien suddenly brought and thrown upon alien airs from some other quarter, but it was conceived along with them, from the first beginning of the world and a fixed part of it, as in us the limbs are seen to be' (Lucretius [1924] 1975. 5: 546–9). The earth is fabricated, no different from plants, forests, stones or ourselves. It is an "individual" in the proper Spinozist sense of the word. An individual that consists of a series of individuals, that is materialized through its relations and that is necessarily in change, that exists in its resonances. For Serres there is no difference between the drying up of the Garonne river and his joints being worn out. Both are equally painful to him, physically and mentally. Both necessarily happen together. And together, they call for new alliances, the search for new nuptials, new trajectories (technical, mechanical, organic, digital), new ideas. *Their shared appetite proves that they are actually 'the same thing'.*

Find the music of the piece within the larger never-ending music of the place! What a great assignment composer John Luther gave to the musicians taking part in his 'comprovisation' *Sila: The Breath Of The World*. Summarized by the relation between the wood and the iron, music is one of those arts that always started from the possible ecologies in which it happened. Oscillating between the wood and the iron, the sky and the earth, the good composer is always telling us, Listen! there are so many other sounds to be un/heard! Sounds that matter/matters that sound. Yet a similar playfulness is, of course, at work in all of the arts. So many other things to be un/seen. So many things to be un/felt. So many earths waiting to be realized.

Change your appetite! To forget critique, to forget Cartesianism, to forget the possible ways to liberate oneself from the crisis that haunt you and, instead, to practice freedom, fully blend into creative geophilosophical exploration through art and philosophy – that is my aim. Let us accept that there is no alternative, or, no difference, no otherness able to release itself from Cartesianism. *There is only wholly otherness.* It is in the immanent mapping of sameness that a new earth immanently arises. Practicing the thinker, producing the artist only asks for another way of perceiving. Imagine otherwise.

Part 2

THIS IS NOT THE EARTH!

Can we welcome the many forms of being that we always already were? It is not an easy task to dehumanize ourselves but by all means a necessary and an urgent one. It is time we face the fact that the earth is not ours, in fact, that we, humans, are nothing but fungi on the face of the earth. Or better: the most destructive life-form the earth has ever hosted.

Rethinking our presence, the key question is: why do so many of our ideas that now dominate the earth, easily qualify for being humanist, or anthropocentric, 'human all too human'? How come they are, by all means, very far removed from the logic of the earth (to which we belong) and *still persevere in being*? We live in a world deeply grooved by complex systems of religion, humanism and capitalism – systems that seem omnipresent and that do not seem to leave us much room to think otherwise. Taking the geometer as my perspective I propose to explore how we are to deal with all that keeps us from opening our eyes again and witnessing the earth. Rereading Reza Negarestani and Michel Tournier especially, our goal is now to let ourselves be opened up by this wholly otherness, or better: *to become a target*.

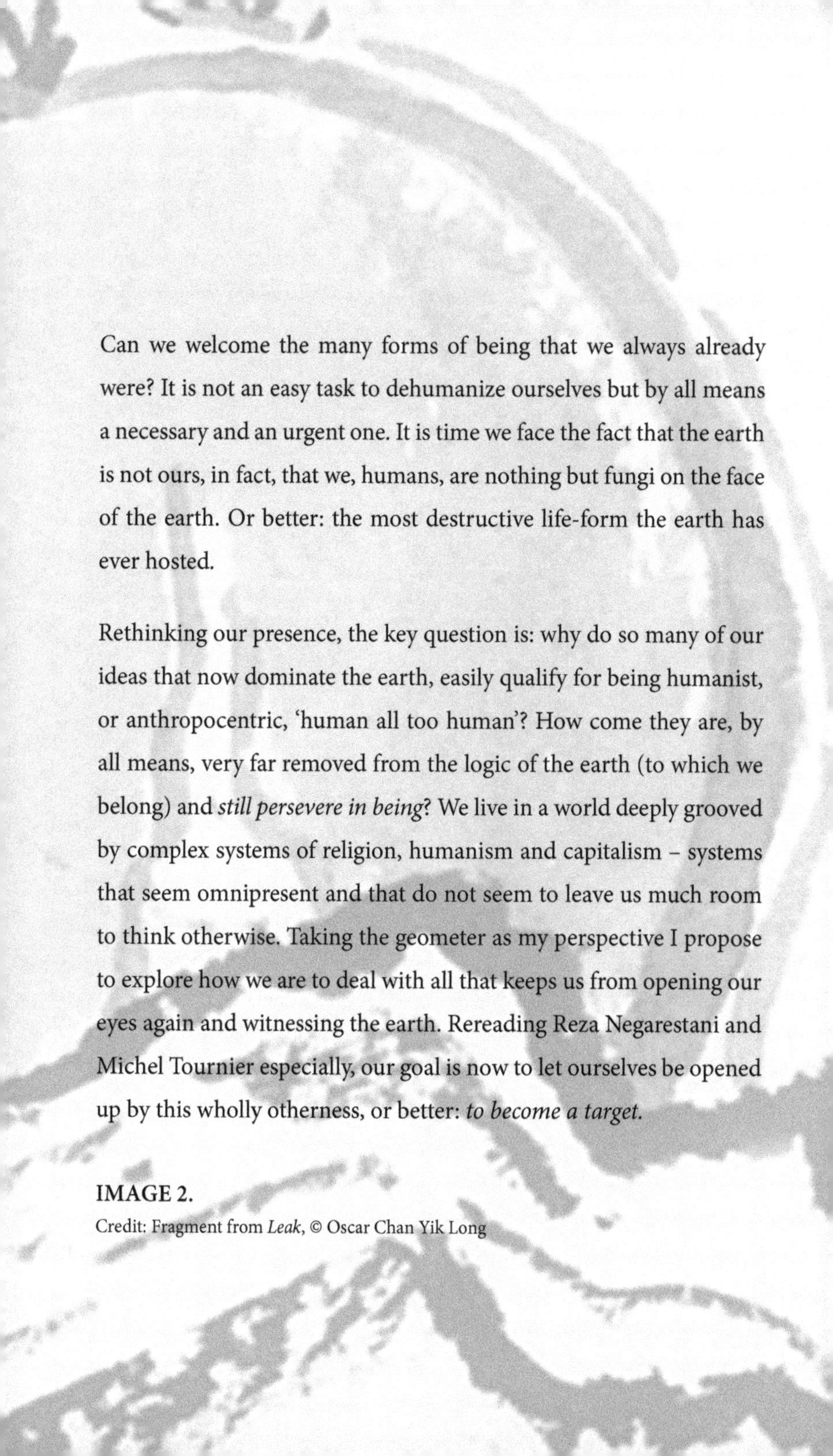

IMAGE 2.
Credit: Fragment from *Leak*, © Oscar Chan Yik Long

The philosopher is the geometer

Geophilosophy starts after the flood retreats, when the water and the land mix and become fertile and 'a new time' announces itself (as Herodotus would put it). What has happened? What to do now? In their chapter of *What Is Philosophy?* entitled 'Geophilosophy', Gilles Deleuze and Félix Guattari explore the new rhythm that emerges when the movements of our bodies and the newly found soil start resonating and functioning together, creating ideas and images, and ultimately, things. They state that 'thinking takes place in the relationship of territory and the earth' ([1991] 1994, 85), which is exactly the task given to geometers when they are exposed to the newfound land. Imagine the thoughts and ideas of geometers, as they feel the tides, the seasons, the winds, as they speculate on new forms of life, territorialize, deterritorialize and reterritorialize! Thinking oscillates between the imagined orders of territory (the Totem) and the chaos of the new earth, full of surprises, unimaginable, beautiful and terrifying at the same time. Territory and the earth are inseparable from the moment that thinking begins; all thought removes itself from a territory, towards the earth, while it is at the same time installing a territory, removing itself from the earth.

To groove the earth, to cultivate it, for that matter, immediately comes with a withdrawal from the earth. As Alfred North Whitehead puts it: '[t]he groove prevents straying across country and the abstraction abstracts from something to which no further attention is paid' (Whitehead [1925] 1967, 197). Grooves are the worldly 'ribs and the rhythms' that we easily slip into, that organize the earth, that territorialize it and, as they remove us from the earth, prevent thinking from happening. We can see this happening all around us. Already at the start of the twentieth century, Whitehead was concerned about us forgetting the earth. He witnessed how industrialization ruined the landscapes of the British Isles he loved so dearly and became very worried about the non-ecological nature of the modern factories (run by steam engines) that lay scattered seemingly randomly across them. Of course, 'randomly' from an environmental perspective, as their machinery functioned independent from anything else forming both the starting point and the paradigm for the products it delivered (to paraphrase Descartes).

Whitehead noticed that the modern factory, as a productive unity in itself, was not in conversation with its surroundings, or, worse, it was only in a seriously unproductive relationship with its environment (the only exchange between them being the 'waste' or the pollution). But it was not the 'technology' as such that he feared (as he considered technology necessarily an abstraction from nature). Rather, he wondered what kind of 'thing' the factory had become. If it was so exclusive, so opposed to its surroundings, what, on earth, made it 'persevere in being'? I dare you to ask yourself the Spinozist question: What is the factory imagining itself to be? What kind of *false ideas* have factories promoted, to such an extent that they (in very different ways, of course) are able to *forget* the earth that imagined them? What happened, *the very moment* these ideas turned out to be so poisonous (for more questions like these, see also Parr 2013)?

Bad ideas sometimes are easy to spot, but always difficult to get rid of. They are always partial, never universal. And they are so for a very good reason, as only by creating difference, by opposing, by grooving, hierarchies come into existence and the dominance they depend on can be realized. Through dominance (hierarchies, differences), a new order can be internalized, like a trauma, the way the Law of the Father has so often done this in the course of history, causing poisonous family relations to persist and to expand. For good reasons, it worried Gregory Bateson that, albeit their zombified (and therefore zombifying) state, unearthly technologies kept on mattering, somehow. Why do bad ideas not simply rot away, drown in their own misery, *like they should*? Why is there something like an ecology of bad ideas? And why do these ecologies of bad ideas (that don't work) still find ways to persist in being?

Similar to how I notice the religious, humanist and capitalist realities of the day persisting in their being, Deleuze and Guattari stress the tripartite power of money, work and housing and how these powers *jointly* keep our current state of zombie-capitalism at work. Contrary to how econometrics and neo-classical (Samuelsonian) blackboard economists (like bad Heads of the Household) reduce these powers to set-theoretical equations (cut loose from the earth), Deleuze and Guattari notice how these three 'bad ideas' overcode and organize the realities we live today. They claim that money, work and housing are the dimensions that dramatically entrench the humanized socioscapes of our age, but just as well give form to the sea, the stratosphere and the desert (cf. [1980] 1987, 481) as we know them. How prophetic! In *Anti-Oedipus* they stress that all of these sociopolitical systems are variations upon systems of alliance and filiation (see [1972] 1984, 146, 192, 196 and 227). They find their point of origin in the household, where, untouched by the eye of the despot, the particular organization of money, work and housing was the root of the household economy.

Perhaps it started when the geometer turned into the economist, the 'he who runs the household', the agoraphobic social scientist who suffers from the perverse need to translate the world according to the simplest lines and numbers. Economy is a tribal invention that started with the circulation of women and that, throughout history, proved itself the ultimate reterritorialization. The family is merely an early consequence of this invention of the house-*hold*. It is the primary 'niche' where a religious, humanist and capitalist rule could proliferate, far away from the social, mental and environmental ecologies, far away from all the non-human others. In the Name of the Father. Not surprisingly, capitalism has always thrived in niches like that.

As such, capitalism (the merchant, the tradesman, all the other early faces of the economist) sought for ways to cooperate with religion (the priest) and humanism (the chief). Capitalism has often found lifelong allies with religion and humanism, but always started from the deterritorialized households. In Hegel, we can read about the dangers of the household and about the need for thought to escape the household's rule; the Father suffocates us, with his claim to normalcy and actively prevents thought from happening. Hegel is right when he emphasizes that the enclosed nature of the household might lead to a situation very hostile to thinking. But normalcy is not the problem. Rather, it is difference, as it is the *privacy* of the household which can possibly give rise to those sites where money, work and housing overcode everything else. Resonating the powers of the priest and the statesman, the Father can reterritorialize everyone and everything within reach, upon the deepest of the grooves, creating a bad ecology, a cancerous body that has the power to expand in all possible directions. Never underestimate the power of a single household – It can turn extremely infectious. Not too long ago, scholars like David Graeber reminded us once again that capitalism is only run by a small number of households, worldwide (also known as 'the 1%'). It has never been different.

In capitalism was never the priest or the chief upon which society got reterritorialized; it was the household (the power of the Father). Money, work and housing, can run the nuclear family, just as it can easily run the factory in all of its zombie-capitalist mutations. Remember that Marx, too, noted that the first division of labour took place in the family (giving birth to children) and that the family held the essence not only of slavery but also of bondage. Marx was also right to conclude that the family has always been the potential miniature of all the dualisms that, in the end, became the main forms of organization of society (Engels [1891] 1976, 75).

The geophilosopher, whose desire it is to always rethink nature at large, has to let itself be deterritorialized by the earth in order to ungroove it – ungrooving in the sense of getting rid of the grooves *and* of finding the ungrooved earth. The time has come to rethink the Earth and the Sun (Gaia and Helios) from the perspective of the

Lady Mother (Demeter) and not from the perspective of the patriarch (Zeus), as Homer already told us. Homer is a native of Ionia – the mythical home of the Spinozist undercurrent – that home between the land and the sea where people from all over the empire moved, giving rise to a society which was not based on established kinship patterns. Ionia is a society with a love for *sophia*, a love for *techne*, where the love of humanity was not based on *nomos* but on *physis* (see Karatani [2012] 2017, 41). Homer's writings still show us how imagination and thought thrive with the search for *a life on a new earth*. Away from the household, a new earth reveals itself, as the most fantastic undercurrents turn real. Isn't it telling that even at the end of the *Odyssey*, Odysseus is once more leaving the household?

It is in this light that I propose to read Quentin Meillassoux's timely 'critique upon the Critique': his speculative materialist critique upon the horror of philosophy which he named the humanism of Immanuel Kant. In an attempt to free thought from the 'finitude', from the grooves in which thought has become stranded, Meillassoux is continuing this Spinozist line of thinking, especially when he stresses that nature can very well be known (absolutely) – contrary to how Kantian dualism has always considered nature to be thinkable but unknowable: in other words, 'doomed' to be stuck in humanist narratives. In *After Finitude: An Essay on the Necessity of Contingency*, Meillassoux ([2006] 2008) starts his anti-metaphysics (as he calls it) with an interest in 'ancestrality', a phrase that he uses to refer to all realities before they appeared to humanity or actually any form of life on earth, or 'diachronicity' (a term he introduces later in the book and which concerns the events after human life or life on earth) and in the 'arche-fossil', those materials that index the existence of an ancestral reality.

Meillassoux searches for 'the great outdoors': the absolute outside which is anterior or posterior to life (or thought) and which thus wards off the possibility of grooving. Moving away from Kantian ideas of consciousness which are only interested in how objects appear for and to us (as in, fully embedded in the grooves we have created), clearly a rewriting of the Cartesian model of thought, Meillassoux wants to free thinking through the earth, or as he puts it (Meillassoux, [2006] 2008):

> And if contemporary philosophers insist so adamantly that thought is entirely oriented towards the outside, this could be because of their failure to come to terms with a bereavement – the denial of a loss concomitant with the abandonment of dogmatism. The great outdoors, the absolute outside of pre-critical thinkers: that outside which was not relative to us, and which was given as indifferent to its own givenness to be what it is, existing in itself regardless of whether we are thinking of it or not; that outside which thought could explore with the legitimate feeling of being on foreign territory – of being entirely elsewhere.
>
> (7)

The idea of being 'on foreign territory', as stated above, of being confronted with grooves that are not familiar to us or perhaps even with an elsewhere which has not been grooved at all (because it has not been grooved, or because it cannot be), is a major challenge to philosophy because it means that philosophy must sacrifice its greatest possession: consciousness and its language as the essential point of departure for thinking about the world. Meillassoux is here more radical than Nietzsche when he considers the necessity of forgetting to be only the first (superficial) step to take in order to come to a philosophy that is not limited by human (Kantian) finitude, by the grooves we created, to a geophilosophy that, in the end, is indeed earthlier. Only when philosophy accepts that 'the same cause may actually bring about "a hundred different events"' (Meillassoux [2006] 2008, 90), it can begin to fulfil its task, which is to take into account all of those consequences that refuse to be understood, that refuse to act according to our terms.

The Deserted ...

A direct answer to Meillassoux's ancestrality and diachronicity, his search for *the Great Outdoors* and his interest in foreign territories or ungrooved 'entirely elsewheres', can be found in Deleuze's earliest published text, *Desert Islands*, which came out in 1953. Anticipating Meillassoux, Deleuze starts by telling us that 'islands are either from before or for after humankind' ([2002] 2004, 9). Thus, he is interested in what we may refer to as 'the unterritorialized' (which could be that space not yet inhabited but just as well the space being smoothened, given back to the earth again), that millisecond before thinking starts *and* just after it has stopped. A thinking that refuses to be present.

Deleuze starts his career by searching for the kind of thought that 'happens' at the unterritorialized. In *A Thousand Plateaus*, this kind of thinking is famously referred to as 'nomad thought', where Deleuze and Guattari conclude that 'the nomads make the desert no less than they are made by it' (Deleuze and Guattari [1980] 1987, 382). New bodies and minds are being formed in a nomadology. Rosi Braidotti, in her feminism, in her theology and ecology, practices exactly that nomadology, as this allows for a freedom of movement, a freedom of thought, unspoiled by the phallogocentric, Christian and capitalist grooves that had limited our thinking before.

In *Desert Islands*, Deleuze, rudimentarily, plays with territory and the earth as the breeding ground for thought. There, at the horizon, new land arises from the sea, or, a new idea comes about. Far removed from money, work and housing, far removed from the Others, as will be discussed shortly, the deserted island might offer us a new philosophy. A philosophy unfamiliar to subjects and objects, friendly and fraternal.

Of all possible islands, it is above all, the deserted island most of all; it *demands* a most radical dehumanization, as Deleuze calls it throughout this text. The deserted island, even more so than the ancestral and diachronic statement Meillassoux introduced us to, only accepts a full surrender (as we will soon see) in order to be thought, or rather, in order to find out in what way the island would allow thought to be possible in the first place. Lacking territory, the deserted island cannot be thought; it insists on remaining unthought. This means that it is impossible to continue one's life when arriving at the shore of a deserted island. A 'new life' has to be invented with the 'new earth' time and again. In a new life 'there is an extraordinarily fine topology that relies not on points or objects, but rather on haecceities, on sets of relations (winds, undulations of snow or sand, the song of the sand or the creaking of the ice, the tactile qualities of both)' (Deleuze and Guattari [1980] 1987, 382). Thus, the truly deserted island, as Deleuze already concluded in *Desert Islands*, has to be that place from which *thought itself* is created anew: as a necessarily unfixed, unfixing perhaps, variation on the ungrooved, uninhabited earth.

Ideally, then, this is what makes the deserted island such a wonderful and unique place on earth; new lives and new thoughts, radically different from existing lives and thoughts, can be moulded from the deserted (and the unpeopled). It requires a radical reducing of oneself, of the Human Being, before one is able to reach this 'consciousness of the movement which produced the island' (Deleuze [2002] 2004, 10). It is only there, at the deserted island, that one can find

> an Idea of humanity, a prototype, a man who would almost be a god, a woman who would be a goddess, a great Amnesiac, a pure Artist, a consciousness of Earth and Ocean, an enormous hurricane, a beautiful witch, a statue from the Easter Islands. There you have a human being who precedes itself.
>
> (idem, 11)

As far away from the suffocating present as one can be, way after finitude, it is *only* at the deserted island that the Derridean theme 'I am (not) born (yet)' (Derrida and Ewald 2001, 55) can be voiced.

Michel Tournier's novel *Friday* shows us how to think the deserted island and all that it can do. Very much contrary to Daniel Defoe's *Robinson Crusoe*, with its colonialist and racist undertones, Tournier's revitalization of the story offers us a fine manifesto of how the deserted island happens and how it refuses grooving. As in Defoe, Robinson intrudes upon the deserted island (one that, as we soon find out, has always already been inhabited) and (finally) searches for ways to be included in the island's existence. And, again, as in Defoe's novel, this turns out to be extremely difficult. Robinson tries to establish two of the normalities that he took from the modern world (monotheistic religion and capitalism) and – in turn – tries to adapt them to Speranza, the island. The third one – humanism – will in the end prove the most difficult to crack.

Speranza does not 'resist' Robinson's colonization. On the contrary, both normalities actually work very well. Yet, as he installed these alien regimes, the island does not re/veil itself (it did not reveille/reveal/unveil itself). Despite Robinson's efforts (which included actual penetration) no openness was realized; there was no awakening, which explains Robinson's alienation in this first part of the book. Christianity, to start with the first of the two regimes, seems to be simply ignored by the island. In the beginning of the novel, the Bible plays an important role, but gradually it disappears. It is true, as Petit (1991, 10) suggests, that there are interesting parallels between the Bible and this novel as a whole (e.g. that the explosion central to the book marks the switch between the old and the new testaments). Yet, since in the end it does not seem to work, Robinson himself loses interest in Christianizing the island (and Friday).

Or, perhaps it is *through* Friday that Christianity no longer made any sense. Friday is not simply a name Robinson gives to personify an alleged inhumanity that always already lives on (with) the island. Friday necessarily also signals the day of Christ's death, the day of fasting as Robinson notes (Tournier [1967] 1997, 70) and the day of Aphrodite's (Venus) birth (idem, 228). Friday is the foam that washes upon the island and searches for new forms of fertilization. Because of Friday everything changes.

Capitalism, despite its relatively short existence, proves to be an even stronger force than Christianity. Note how Robinson, after a short period of desolation at the beginning of the book, quickly believes in accumulation again. As he notes in his journals: 'Henceforth I shall abide the following rule: all production is creation, therefore good; all consumption is destruction therefore bad... To accumulate!' (Tournier [1967] 1997, 61). But, although rather successful (Robinson collects a huge surplus), even capitalism is eventually abandoned. It takes about half the book before he is capable of resisting it, but quite early in the text, the island itself (later repeated through Friday) already shows Robinson, once and for all, that these imported strategies will not work here:

> There was a radiance in the air; and in a moment of inexpressible happiness Robinson seemed to discern another island behind the one he had laboured so long in solitude, a place more alive, warmer and more fraternal, which his mundane preoccupations had concealed from him.
>
> (Tournier [1967] 1997, 90)

The key term in the above quote is 'another island'. Another island is concealed from Tournier's Robinson: it is impossible. But why is another island impossible for Robinson? Because of Robinson's mundane preoccupations. In his reading of Tournier in *The Logic of Sense*, Deleuze defines the limits of the possible in his conceptualization of 'otherness' (which is opposed to 'anotherness'). Yes, here is humanism – the third normality that Robinson imported (though he was largely unaware of it). The Other explains what these 'mundane preoccupations' may be. Deleuze claims that this is what happens:

> I desire nothing that cannot be seen, thought, or possessed by a possible Other. That is the basis of my desire. It is always Others

who relate my desire to an object.... The other is initially a structure of the perceptual field, without which the entire field could not function as it does.

([1969] 1990, 306-7)

In other words, it is through Others that my desires/appetites are directed, thus continuing (for instance) Christianity and capitalism. Others are the mundane preoccupations that keep Robinson from catching up with the movement of the island prior to humankind, from finding a new form of life.

Deleuze claims that Tournier's novel *Friday* presents 'Robinson: the man without Others on his island' (Deleuze [1969] 1990, 304). In the end, Robinson rids himself of the Others that have haunted him and that, although not actually present, directed his desires, until the island revealed to him 'another island': a place more alive, warmer and fraternal. Tournier's novel tells us how deserted islands reveal their desertedness, their impossible colonization, their ability to wash away all the grooves made in the sand. Speranza shows its islandness, surrounded by the sea that immediately erases all of its inscriptions, that always already ungrooves. Anotherness comes into being through these earthly dynamics so essential for the deserted island. It can only come into being when the Others have vanished.

The pathologists
of the earth

There are many different deserted islands. And they can be found everywhere, but, of course, only where you least expect them. Deserted islands are impossible, or necessarily unforeseen. Reza Negarestani, in his debut *Cyclonopedia: Complicity with Anonymous Materials*, states that the Middle East springs from the Dead Sea. Its deserts refuse to be inhabited, and after being grooved by colonial and postcolonial forces – among them Christianity and (even more so) capitalism – the earthly dynamics are now surfacing from beneath and starting to reveal another island underneath. Contrary to Tournier, whose Robinsonade *Friday* is a novel which 'gives rise' to a rich complex of geophilosophical concepts, Negarestani's work has little to do with the novel form anymore. It is H.P. Lovecraft plus early Greek Chthonic mysticism. It talks of Pazuzu and Ugallu-demons and of Deleuze and Guattari's war machine. It combines astrophysics with the fictional diary of a Hamid Parsani.

Cyclonopedia, in every way, practices the 'radical paranoia – as a speculative line of schizophrenia' (Negarestani 2008, 220). Yet it is in this form of madness, which is impossible to summarize, that the Middle East reveals an anotherness: a world more alive, friendlier and more fraternal. It is a world that suffers, that continues to be ridden by extreme violence in many ways, but that slowly and gently finds a way of undying. It has already started to wash away the alien (Occidental, post-Kantian) grooves that had been overcoding its space for so long. Such is the world after 9/11, the explosion in the middle that marks capitalism's new stage (which might nevertheless last for eternity) and that has shaken the earth as a whole: all of its deserted islands and the seas that surround them (for instance, the Arab Spring and the Occupy movement).

Like Tournier, Negarestani is convinced that the process of dehumanization has set in with the ultimate desert(ed). Tournier refers to the ultimate desert(ed) as Speranza, Negarestani talks of Xerodrome, or the Tellurian Omega: that which has presented itself as 'another island' to Robinson and which is at work beneath Speranza is also at work underneath the Middle East. Negarestani shows how a politics of space (Deleuze/Guattari's ecosophical or geophilosophical search for a new earth) necessarily comes with an ungrooving of colonial/postcolonial ribs and rhythms that cover up the Middle East, similar to the way in which Speranza had to be released from Robinson's colonizing efforts.

It is this geophilosophy that Negarestani's main character in *Cyclonopedia*, Hamid Parsani, develops as his 'philosophy of oil'. Parsani is an Iranian archaeologist, who, before disappearing under mysterious circumstances (later he reappears again), convinces us that the philosophy of oil can re/veil the mighty undercurrents of the Middle East. He notices that the oil is the speechless and consciousness-less physical spirit that opens up the body of the island Asia Minor. Oil, he claims, by now greasing Integrated World Capitalism (as Félix Guattari would refer to it), recomposes its flows accordingly. Yet only recently (in the wake of 9/11) oil has started to realize the entirely 'new landscape' we find ourselves in today. With the accident, with 9/11, the Big Bang in the middle, its Furies were satisfied and slowly and kindly a new earth can come into being.

Although discernible only on a hidden level, *Cyclonopedia* demands the collapse of the two major systems of grooving that we saw in Tournier's *Friday*: capitalism and religion. Parsani first of all talks of the Gods, who must die. Or rather, they ought to take solar voyages to the earthly ground to become dead Gods. But what do dead Gods do? Parsani explains:

> The dead god is not a tired, abolished or doomed god but a god with its ultimate weapon of catastrophic devastation. A plague coming to earth to make of the earth's restrictive ground a direct passage to openness, the dead god mortifies itself by affirming the earthly ground within which it is buried. If the act of descent, as associated with dead gods, is identified as the secularization of the divine's body (departing from the divine's sovereignty), the dead god itself is by no means a secular entity. In the process of descending, the dead god rediscovers its supposedly secular corpus as a pestilential but love-saturated communion with the sacred. Through descent, the god commits a crime at once secular and sacred: It opens itself by eating and infecting the human, and opens the human by turning itself into a corpse.

> (Negarestani 2008, 204–5)

It is hardly surprising that the death of God affects us all, matters to us all, flows under our skin. The dead Gods, the Chthonic Deities from beneath the surface of the earth, fertilize the land, vitalize it again, smoothening the alien grooves that had organized its surface including the humans that never really inhabited it. Let's face it, they had to kill *all* of their Gods, as the scripture/the prophesy always already told us: a new world awaits.

With the killing, Negarestani notes, a new earthly economy has to be reinvented: 'According to Parsani, the Earth always plays the role of the subversive Insider against the Empire of the Sun, which has given rise to terrestrial orders, politics and modes of living based on hegemonic stardom' (Negarestani 2008, 42). And it is this economy, he claims, a molecular economy that has nothing to do with present-day capitalism, that is currently starting to rise from the Middle East.

> In his interview, Parsani suggests that the Middle East has simulated the mechanisms of dusting to mesh together an economy which operates through positive degenerating processes, an economy whose carriers must be extremely nomadic, yet must also bear an ambivalent tendency towards the established system or the ground. An economy whose vehicle and systems never cease to degenerate themselves. For in this way, they ensure their permanent molecular dynamism, their contagious distribution and diffusion over their entire economy.
>
> (Negarestani 2008, 91)

Yet, this religious and economic revolution is not a humanist development; it is not consequential to otherness. It arises from a non-human other, from wholly otherness, from oil; this heaviest of the hydrocarbons that flows rapidly, in every direction underneath its soil, is the essence of the Middle East. Negarestani follows geophysicist Thomas Gold's theory of the Deep Hot Biosphere. He claims that

> petroleum is not a fossil fuel, and that oil has its origin in natural gas flows which feed bacteria living in the bowels of the earth. Therefore, the demonarchy of oil is not subjected to the laws of the dead (i.e. the preserved corpses of prehistoric organisms) but rather is animated by a Plutonic vitalism (abiogenic petroleum generated by nether biosphere of the earth... rather than from decomposition of fossils and organic body-counts. Consequently, oil is far more substantial and follows a different, autonomous logic of planetary distribution.
>
> (2008, 72)

Full of new forms of life, but consisting solely of highly condensed dead organic compounds, oil, Parsani concludes, is everywhere. Or, as Negarestani tells us: 'Books, foods, religions, numbers, specks of dust – all are linguistically, geologically, politically and mathematically combined into petroleum. For him, everything is suspiciously oily' (2008, 42). Surfacing at the deserted island called the Middle East, oil is the undead capable of virtually vitalizing everything.

Negarestani's search for a new life offered to us by the earth, for the oily undead, the subversive Insider, is precisely the search, or rather the flow, that Robinson, near the end of Tournier's novel, started to live. The feeling of being in a place more alive, friendlier and more fraternal, or better, being given the power to create one's life on another island, to rise from its soil, is crucial here. Both Negarestani and Tournier take up the Nietzschean challenge to play the role of the pathologist of the earth. They search for a health, similar to Nietzsche (remember that the latter, until the very end, in *Ecce Homo*, insisted that he was actually very healthy (and rightfully so!)). Yet, it could well be phrased the other way around. For, to evoke Artaud (and, in doing so, to do justice to Negarestani), I could also claim that we are searching for 'a real sickness... which touches the essence of being... [and which] applies to a whole life' (Artaud 1976, 44). It is a Great Health *and* a real sickness that the earth has to offer us, one enfolded in the other, ad infinitum.

This earthly health/sickness has to be acquired over and over again because one is continuously required to sacrifice it. It is a health/sickness of people 'who are often shipwrecked and bruised', as Nietzsche put it. They are people who are dangerously healthy/sick and who find before them

> a country still undiscovered, the horizon of which no one has yet seen, a beyond to every country and every refuge of the idea that man has ever known, a world so overflowing with beauty, strangeness, doubt, terror, and divinity, that both our curiosity and our lust of possession are frantic with eagerness.
>
> ([1908] 2009, 100)

In the topological art of moving between health and sickness, Robinson's striving to catch up with the movements of the island, the wind, the power of the sun, was the creative act that gave him his earthly health/sickness and which, in turn, made him 'live perpetually in a moment of innocence' (Deleuze [1969] 1990, 205), as Tournier writes. As if he had witnessed the hidden treasure chambers of the Mesopotamian necropolises opening up their overwhelmingly different fields of distribution.

Become a target

The experience of death is neither life's denial nor its absence (death is not 'the other' of life). On the contrary: it has always already been the essence of every living thing much more so than life. Spinoza the Stoic had already taught us that the experience of death is the first and foremost reason for any individual (an island, a Robinson, any possible ecology) to persevere in its being, constantly searching for ways to revitalize the relations between the individuals of which one is made. With Spinoza, the claim that the free thinks of death the least of all things (cf. E4P67) does not mean that one's unity is not haunted by death, but rather that the free equals the creative who constantly finds new ways to free themselves from grooves that limited their being. Death, therefore, is by all means enveloped into the core of every individuality. It gives birth to its creation. Death is the humus; it resides in the bowels of the earth from which everything stems, pushing everything in the direction of the sun (life). It opens up the individuality carrying life; it opens and infects the individual, creating life anew. Death eats its way through everything, creating the strings of matter which life lives.

The plurality of forms demands death (even more so than madness and sickness) to happen, demands that man lets himself be killed. Only then, new thoughts and new lives happen, lives that are not harassed by the Others' organization of our bodies. Tournier's another island, from which Deleuze conceptualized 'anotherness' as a radically different strategy from 'otherness', is all about rejecting the existence of man-and-his-changing-relationships-with-the-earth. Instead, anotherness is about *prioritizing* the event, or perhaps even prioritizing (death and) life itself, to give form to 'a life' (amongst many others) as a series of non-essential features. Negarestani, on the other hand, talks of a complicity with anonymous materials (which is the subtitle of *Cyclonopedia*) by which he emphasizes the closedness of the necrocratic regime.

When Robinson searched to create a new earth, a new style of life, he was keen on inventing a possibility of life, on exploring a way of existing. Near the end of the book, Robinson ended up a *result* of circumstances on the desert island, which meant that he and everything he embodied had emerged from the island's ecology. The island gave him his second, non-carnal birth! But in order to realize that, he first had to die. He had to be taken over by the island. He had to be eaten and infected by Speranza, and he had to allow that to happen. He had to become a target for Speranza.

To become a target is what Negarestani keeps referring to with his neologism 'polytics', his term to replace 'politics', which has become too infected with post-1968 philosophies of Otherness. It is no doubt the most important argument of the book and definitely demands much more attention from theory in the near future (if only because it has become the political agenda of the Arab Spring and the Occupy (yellow umbrella) movement and the anti-extradition law movement that vitalized Hong Kong in 2019). Becoming a target comes close to what our main character, Hamid Parsani, in his numerous publications, has referred to as 'the enigma of openness', which is to lie at the heart of polytics. The enigma of openness, Parsani tells us, is that true openness involves a radical closedness, as is made clear in the following example of 'love':

> The openness associated with love is itself a yet stronger closure to the outside world. Between two lovers, openness is initially established to close them upon themselves and from the outside. Love (philia) in all its forms entangles openness with closure, and ultimately closure with the radical exteriority of the outside, from which only impossibility actively emanates: the impossibility of being closed as well as the impossibility of affording the outside.
>
> (2008, 220)

The enigma of openness, this inverse mechanism of complicity, summarizes Deleuze's anotherness, Tournier's another island, Meillassoux's Deleuzianism and, above all, the polytics that Negarestani himself proposes. It comes down to the idea that true revolution, true change, is about being opened (by) rather than being open (to) (cf. for instance Negarestani 2008, 242 and 2011a, 15). Presented by Negarestani as a continuation of Deleuze and Guattari's politics of becoming (cf. 2008, 196), polytics calls for an ecology of *clopenness* (a term from topology combining closed and open), which does not start from language, conscience or even man (and his Other) but from a need to become a target, from a need to be opened up (by).

Negarestani summarizes the power of 'being opened (by)':

'I am open to you' can be recapitulated as 'I have the capacity to bear your investment' or 'I afford you'. This conservative voice is not associated with will or attention but with the inevitability of affordance as a mesophilic bond, and with the survival economy and the logic of capacity. If you exceed the capacity by which you can be afforded, I will be cracked, lacerated and laid open. Despite its dedication to repression, its blind desire for the monopoly of survival and the authoritarian logic of the boundary, the plane of 'being open to' has never been openly associated with paranoia and regression. Such is the irony of liberalism and anthropomorphic desire.

(2008, 198)

To be 'opened up by' is the invention, the moment of creation, the accident that just has to happen: it brings forth the possibility of a wholly other life. The idea of 'being opened (by), not being open (to)' suggests the ways in which the politics of 'anotherness' can be understood to replace that of 'otherness'.

For Negarestani, the politics of Otherness has haunted the postcolonial discourse of, in his case, the Middle East (think of Edward Said) for too long. Deleuze's rejection of the Other in *The Logic of Sense* already emphasizes the 'being opened (by)', most notably in the way he puts so much emphasis on the moment that Robinson realizes that he has forgotten the Others: 'Those lights have vanished from my consciousness. For a long time, fed by my fantasy, they continued to reach me. Now it is over and the darkness has closed in' (Tournier in Deleuze [1969] 1990, 309). The light, the *zeitgeber* that determines day and night, the seasons and one's geophysical location, humanism in all of its appearances, is no longer there. In the darkness, he experiments with another island that is alive, friendlier and more fraternal.

'Anotherness' has nothing to do with the Other. Read Derrida's *Of Hospitality*: 'absolute hospitality requires that I open up my home and that I give not only to the foreigner (provided with a family name, with the social status of being a foreigner, etc.), but to the absolute, unknown, anonymous other' (Derrida and Dufourmantelles [1997] 2000, 25). Like Derrida, Said himself, by staging the Orient as Europe's Other (Said 1979, 1), both questions and broadens the correlation. But are both not talking only about 'being open to' and not about 'being opened by'? Derrida still talks of the (Cartesian and) Kantian Subject when he himself opens his own house, in the same way that Said envisions Europe opening itself up to the Orient.

Is not this exactly the kind of humanism or anthropocentrism that Negarestani, Deleuze, but also Tournier are trying to get rid of? And is not this Deleuzian 'anotherness', this Negarestanian polytics or, rather, this Robinsonian 'another island', this Parsanian 'philosophy of oil' by all means offering us that very different revolution, a Spinozist one, a materialist one? Negarestani is fierce in his rejection of the Other: 'To become open, or to experience the chemistry of openness is not possible through "opening yourself".… Radical openness can be evoked by becoming more of a target for the outside… one must seduce the exterior forces of the outside' (2008, 199).

Anotherness does not presume a Self that is or is not sympathetic to an Other, to an outside. Negarestani's polytics is the radical outside. Thus, this New Earth (as Deleuze and Guattari present it in *Anti-Oedipus*) can also never be *of* the earth (it cannot be its property). As Negarestani puts it: 'Deleuze and Guattari's slyly appropriated

"New Earth" presents a model of an earth whose every surface and trellis is an unground, a terminal planetary body tolerating neither solar economies nor its own terrestriality' (2008, 43). Indeed, the New Earth is being opened (by), not being open (to). It does not tolerate anything (religion, humanism, capitalism), not even the earth itself. It resists the present and its normalities as a whole. It is opened by its unknown undercurrents as they secretly flow in all directions, creating transversals ad infinitum.

This mythological dream for undercurrents holds true not only for the body of the island but equally for Robinson himself, who, when in a state of almost pure joy, is himself opened up by an earthly health/ sickness coming from underneath:

> He pictured his own lungs growing outside himself like a blossoming of purple-tinted flesh, living polyparies of coral with pink membranes, sponges of human tissue.... He would flaunt that intricate efflorescence, that bouquet of fleshy flowers, in the wide air, while a tide of purple ecstasy flowed into his body on a stream of crimson blood.
>
> (Tournier [1967] 1997, 193–4)

Negarestani in a similar way celebrates 'necrocracy', claiming that 'necrocracy suggests the strictures of the conservative economy not in regard to life but in regard to ways the organism dies; and it is the way of returning to the originary death that prescribes the course of life for the organism' (Negarestani 2011b, 192). Getting rid of the organs, of the grooves that order, death is the only way out: 'necrocracy suggests that the organism must die or bind the precursor exteriority only in ways that its conservative conditions or economic order can afford' (Negarestani 2011b, 193).

Negarestani's polytics, in the end, opts for a new understanding of life, posing the question 'if life is the source of living then why do we need to survive?' (2008, 210). For once we realize that the ethics of life is external to that of survival and that survival is a means of resistance to the epidemic and overpowering presence of life, we must conclude that to be pro-life is, essentially, to be anti-survival. Or as Negarestani concludes: 'when it comes to the exteriority of life to the living being, survival is intrinsically impossible' (2008, 210).

Negarestani's 'radical paranoia' resists the continuation of life (as survival): 'Closed and folded in upon itself, radical paranoia is a speculative line of schizophrenia that no longer believes in openness to the outside, since for the living being the outside is merely a vitalistic environment' (2008, 219). The outside then is Otherness; it is a possible world that, Negarestani insists, reinstalls the regimes that we have always known. This is then survival as we knew it: it is Defoe's Robinson who insists on staying alive (staying true to the capitalist and religious grooves he lived in). Then, '[t]o be part of the environment (viz. the economical outside) is to survive' (Negarestani 2008, 219).

Negarestani is onto something different. We have already rejected otherness and its ethical need to be 'open to' as it was promoted in work in the writings of Jacques Derrida and Edward Said. Now Negarestani also rejects Derrida's claim that there is nothing outside context. On the contrary, he seems to urge us to get rid of all possible contextualization. Unlike deconstruction then, radical paranoia opts for

a detachment of itself from the economical outside (the environment) for and by which survival becomes possible.... Radical paranoia reforges survival as that which can sunder the correlation between the paranoia of the living (survival) and economical openness and therefore end its own repression in regard to the unaffordable outside. In radical paranoia, survival is no longer a parasitic (mutually beneficial) symptom of affordability and economical openness, but an event which is disobedient to its vitalistic ambitions.

(2008, 219)

Or to conclude, as Negarestani says, '[t]he separation of survival from openness offers survival the opportunity to act strategically on behalf of radical exteriority and its refractory impossibility' (2008, 220).

We could pose this question (Why do you need to survive?) directly to Robinson, the moment he sets foot on Speranza. It was in this moment that Robinson immediately understood that 'this place was wholly alien and hostile... his boat... was his only link with life' (Tournier [1967] 1997, 36–7). Robinson knew he had first to die in order to realize a new type of living, in order to find his earthly health/ sickness. Death was his only route towards sustainability, to pick up the movement of the island prior to humankind, to be released from religion and capitalism, to be released from the others, from the mundane preoccupations that turn us into minds in a groove. 'A ground swell set in; the beach was a roar with incoming waves; the sea-lice and Django bugs scurried for high ground' (Mishama [1956] 2000, 64).

The oceans had to devour his boat, let it sink to the bottom of the sea, *without leaving a ripple at its surface.*

Part 3

I CAN SEE SOMETHING

It is time to introduce the central theme of the book, being *the crack that opens the earth/the wound that opens the body*. Much anticipated upon in the preceding parts, I will pursue not by defining but by exploring or mapping what the crack can do. More than before, this part of my meditation depends on the work of Haruki Murakami because I read the crack as the central concept in his novels, or maybe better, as its actual cause. In Murakami, everything starts from the crack, the openness or the nothingness that forces us to act as one, to overcome our differences, to think together.

Not the opposition between the object and the subject but the continuation that connects the crack with the wound is key to the philosophy of matter I am proposing. The geometer, the figure introduced in the second part of this meditation, keeps on setting the pace. Roaming the shores that continue to give form to both the land and the sea, the geometer is now accompanied with the figures that Murakami introduces to us, as they come with their shadows and guide us through the undercurrents of life. There, we find cracks and wounds. No one has summarized the importance of the wound more beautifully than the poet Joë Bousquet, who told us, 'My wound existed before me, I was born to embody it' (in Deleuze [1969] 1990, 148) and 'Become the man of your misfortunes; learn to embody their perfection and brilliance' (idem, 149). Keeping this in mind, I propose to continue my thoughts by taking the crack, the wound, as the start of my materialism.

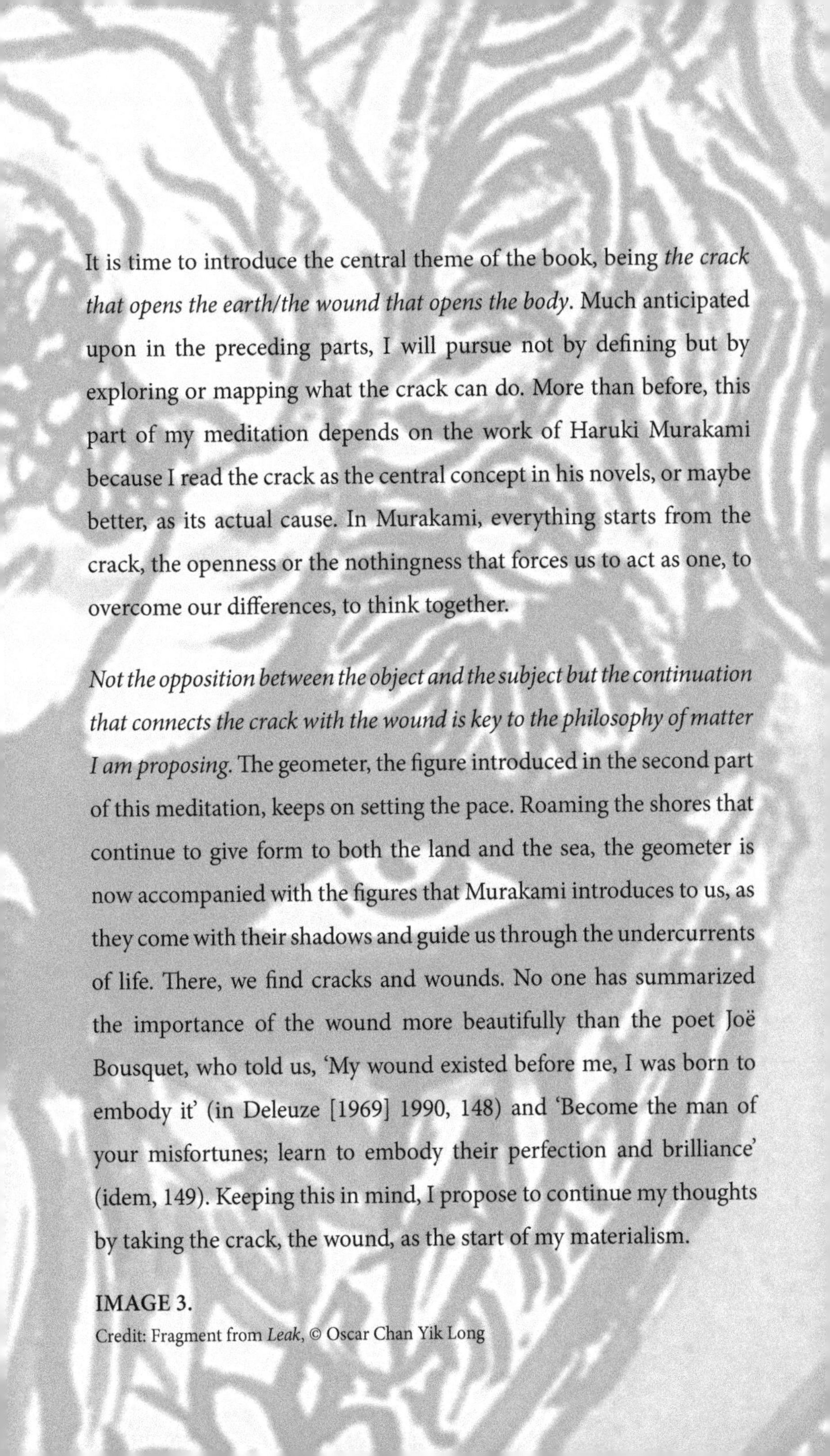

IMAGE 3.

Credit: Fragment from *Leak*, © Oscar Chan Yik Long

I am not a person, right?

Haruki Murakami knows about surfaces and undercurrents, about territories and the earth. From his earliest works he has proven himself a skilful Spinozist geometer, more than weary of the topological possibilities of space and time. In *The Elephant Vanishes*, for instance, we find ourselves in a suburb where the only attraction of a former zoo is an elephant that somehow disappears with its caretaker (which was impossible, considering the size of the elephant and the routes available). Similar to how H.P. Lovecraft, in his first short stories, experiments with an unknown and unknowable (for untraceable) secret of a 'clopen' Piranesi-like interiority (think of his *The Music of Erich Zann*) – an interiority that is both open and closed – the early Murakami, too, circles around such a single crack in the world, a wormhole or a vacuum solution that announces the existence of another earth.

Later in his oeuvre, however, the crack is not placed centre stage, but rather seems to be absolutized in the sense that it is no longer the oddity anymore. Instead, the crack is *solely responsible* for the wholly other earth that we live in. In his trilogy, *1Q84*, this anotherness (established by the Little People) breathes into every possible space (from Tokyo to Chikura) as for instance the sky now always carries two moons: the moon we have always known is now accompanied by a small, green and hideous moon that haunts it, just like the mothers are haunted by the daughters and the 'pupa of air' haunts everybody because its power to duplicate everyone everywhere.

This will change everything, or, everything has already changed.

This second moon affirms to us that, as of now, at least since the year *1Q84* (*another* 1984, as Deleuze would have had it), the dark and connective undercurrents are at work everywhere; they shimmer in all the figures, in all the buildings and in all the words that give form to the staged surface. Together, these figures form a variation of shadows, heavy shadows against light shadows, as Tanizaki would say, that overlap, intersect, create new forms and play with other surfaces. In *1Q84* the presence of another surface turned absolute, but it was especially in Murakami's most celebrated novel *Kafka on the Shore* that the felt presence of anotherness was actively writing itself into every scene. More than that, it was in this book, this doubled portrait, that Murakami shows us how the geometer always already offers us a wholly other idea of subjectivity, a wholly other way to imagine the world otherwise.

The mappings in *Kafka on the Shore* are executed by Kafka Tumura and Nakata Satoru, the two figures that travel (from Tokyo to Takematsu), but not together (so it seems). As always with Murakami, the main characters do not possess details that are developed 'in detail'; rather, as figures, their travels function as media (transformations) to the story in the Simondonian sense: they personify 'the clinching into synergistic relation of a diversity of elements' (Massumi 2009a, 43), as this makes up a situation. Murakami's figures do not function as 'perspectives' from which the story unfolds. They are not relative to 'other elements' that should be of our concern. As with the axonometric landscapes of ukiyo-e artist Ando Hiroshige (1797–1858), who famously painted the fifty-three stops of the Tokaido (the main road between Edo (Tokyo) and Kyoto), the travels reveal spaces that extend themselves along a myriad of bodies, all equally important, equally illuminated, or better, equally emerging as pale light from the shadows that surround them. And only through Kafka and Nakata, the noir doubles of Ikku's Yaji and Kita, do these synergistic relations enter their absolute deterritorialization.

In *Kafka on the Shore*, the story folds back and forth through alternating chapters in which either Kafka (the uneven chapters) or Nakata (the even chapters) figures at centre stage. They cannot meet one another but accompany each other as if they walk on two sides of the same coin: un-present, yet real in their consequences. At the same time, however, and because they seem to be pursuing their journey so differently, their stories have nothing to do with one another. In other words: the doubled chapters per/form a different mode of being and yet they are one (and the same).

Kafka Tumura, also known as 'The Boy Named Crow' (Kafka means 'crow' in Czech), flies through the air, quickly moving from one place to the other in straight lines, always in a rush to get inside and to stay inside: from the inside of the library to the inside of the house in the forest and back again, Kafka is in search for a place to shelter. Throughout the book, he hopes to create a 'new home', to create an environment so safe that 'the function of the real and the function of the unreal are made to co-operate' (Bachelard 1969, xxxi).

Because they don't, in his life. And this non-cooperation frightens him to death. Kafka's search is a search for a home that allows for the living spirits, the *ikiryō* as the Japanese call them, to come about. Finding a new home is the goal of all his travels, as, again, Bachelard concludes: 'the house shelters daydreaming, the house protects the dreamer, the house allows one to dream in peace' ([1958] 1969, 60).

Kafka's journey makes up the major plot. His urge to shelter makes up for the dominant 'progress narrative' of the whole book, in terms of both how his fears originate and in how he solves his paranoia. As could be expected, the abusive father and the loved mother play a key role in this trip ('*mazakon*' is actually a famous Japanese concept for Oedipus complex, coming from the English the 'mother com(plex)'). Written between these two poles – and it is only halfway through the book that the poles unfold – this abusive Father (history) and this loving Mother (future) sediment themselves in the plot (the critical taking-form of the present) as Kafka (the medium) creates both the historical problem (the dark father) and its future solution (the enlightened mother) at the same time.

Kafka's way to navigate between these matters is that he starts to position them via what is then still his omniscient superego, 'The Boy Named Crow'. Starting from the first page of the book in which he packs his bags to leave the house that he considered always already dead, his insecurity is expressed through these internal conflicts, which he overcomes more and more in his traveling, when moving further away from this shameful past and finding the ultimate shelter in the womb of Miss Saeki, who is herself both a fifteen-year-old living spirit and a woman in her fifties whom Kafka believes to be his mother. It is in this ultimate interiority – the womb of Miss Saeki – that Kafka finally finds his peace. The end of his journey, his death, gives him this place which could best be described as 'stable, unmoving, intangible, untouched and almost untouchable, unchanging, deep-rooted' (Perec 1999, 91).

The second main character, Nakata Satoru, known for his ability to talk to cats, crawls his way through the urban fabric. With Nakata, Murakami makes reference to Natsume Soseki's 1905 fantasy *I Am a Cat*, and whereas Kafka is in many ways a crow, the medium, Nakata time and again proves himself to be a cat. Thus, when Kafka flies away from the house that was never a home, from the city of Takamatsu, because he needs to take shelter from the unimaginable dark, Nakata on the other hand, drawn by instinct and movement, always crawls further and further from/in/to the city of Nakano not because he flees but because he is always already hunting for 'an important thing on the right place'.

This is what makes the two main characters *impossible* to each other. Kafka is caught up in the present and all the struggles that define it; he is drawn by a fear (a critique?) of the present but is unable to escape from it. Nakata, on the other hand, doesn't have a present. Nakata, the joyful, inventive cat, is way too clever, too fast and too powerful to be caught in time. Nakata accompanies time, traverses it once in a while (with a smile/as a smile), arises from and dissolves into the darkness again. Unaware of a past and of a future, Nakata's intervention, nevertheless, changes everything.

This happens, for instance, when he actually finds the important thing at the right place near the end of the book. This important thing turns out to be 'the entrance stone', with which he learns to talk. We find out that the entrapment of Kafka (on this side) and of Nakata (on the other side) thus coincides with the entrance stone (although there is in no way a symmetry between them). After Nakata turned the stone, free movement between 'this side' and the 'other side' presumably liberates them both.

The reason for Nakata's life 'on the other side' is explained in top-secret files of the US Department of Defence, in the beginning of the book. They tell us that Nakata as a child has experienced the 'unimaginable light'. In 1944, a group of sixteen schoolchildren inexplicably 'lost consciousness' during an outing (picking mushrooms) in a rural mountain area and only Nakata never really 'got over it'; he never returned to the city where he came from and presumably got his government sub-city, as he calls it himself (Nakata is incapable of reading and writing), as a consequence of this 'accident'. Later in the book the teacher tells different stories which seem to hint at a Freudian explanation again (saying that domestic violence caused Nakata to act differently from her other pupils).

It is tempting to conclude that figures like Kafka and Nakata 'slide into one another', in a Freudian way. Murakami has read Freud and definitely has great sympathy for psychoanalysis, but since his 'pairs' (Kafka and Nakata, the real and the unreal, the light and the dark) rather happen in resonance with one another, are a-causal yet extremely meaningful cross-connections, his world comes closer to what C. G. Jung (1960) has called 'synchronicity', a term Murakami himself has also used (see Murakami [2010] 2012, 1070, 382). Kafka and Nakata live synchronous in that they somehow *imagine* one another vividly. Murakami's figures, always doubled, perform a carefully choreographed dance in their impossible interaction. The travels of Kafka and Nakata do not proceed through a psychoanalytic (re)discovery or (re)distribution of a traumatic past. A history is sometimes reassembled again, but never in order to trace the cause of what happens. Rather, history is a consequence of yet another unknown space. History is a means to explain surfaces being formed. History is what Keiji Nishitani would refer to as 'recovery' (1982, 65).

Recovery suggests regarding what has happened as an active process of both restoring and covering up. Recovery is an ongoing process of realization that happens with the times, and it follows from the relation, from what we must refer to as intra-action. In line with long traditions in (Zen) Buddhist thinking (but reminding us, for instance, of contemporary quantum mechanics, as I discuss this elsewhere in this book), Nishitani's phenomenology stresses that 'what matters is what happens between'. As such the figures composed by Murakami should also be seen as mere consequences of what happens. Nishitani would emphasize their 'nothingness': 'because all the activities of man become manifest as themselves only in unison with absolute nothingness. And yet precisely at this point they are seen to be the most real of realities because they are nothing other than the manifestation of absolute selfhood' (Nishitani 1982, 73).

Starting from the idea that what matters is what happens between, all the persons, all the things, all the figures (I prefer this term) Murakami composes are consequential to the relation. Only in their togetherness, Kafka and Nakata recover urban spheres, forests and all outskirts and backstreets of the city of Takamatsu, where the damned seem to rule. Here, they offer us unreal, dreamlike and vicious characters such as Colonel Sanders and Johnny Walker, figures that recover so many histories, that were now given 'a life' and evil and vicious life, in both cases. And they are well aware of their fantastic recoveries, as the (pimp) Colonel Sanders ensures us: 'I am not a person, okay? How many times do I have to tell you that?… Pimping's just a means of getting you here… I don't have any form… I don't have substance. I'm an abstract concept' (Murakami [2002] 2005, 285).

When Murakami himself claims that all of his writings have a genuine amount of 'real' and 'unreal' in it (in Gabriel, 122), can we say that the real is Kafka and the unreal is Nakata, that the real is the light and the unreal is the darkness? Can we say that the real concerns the abusive Father, the loved mother and above all the fear that flies us from the one to the other and back again. The unreal, crawling in the dark, is the undercurrent, very much active in the real, intervening in it when least expected.

Also, it is the unreal that turns the stone.

Shadows in shadows

In Murakami's stories, the Genesis is not about defining an intrinsic difference between the light and the dark; his chiaroscuro always concerns the play of shadows, which knows no portraits, but only shows us 'the scaping of scapes'. Also, in the end, Murakami does not work with characters, with specific traits and sets of qualities. What happens rather is that, from the first to the last page, he writes *the earthly processes of figuring*. Woven between the different shadows, his narratives are marbling processes, where everything takes place but nothing actually happens. The stories themselves do not progress.

As already mentioned, Kafka's desire/fear to 'get in' is mirrored by Nakata's desire/curiosity to break out. Their synchronicity reveals two modes of the same breath. Or in Milan Kundera's terms ([1983] 2009): Kafka is the one (the bird) has to become the one who perpetually falls inside (heaviness, the darkness), whereas Nakata (the cat) has to become the one who has to climb out, towards the light, never afraid of falling (lightness). Again, they are – in Spinozist terms – the same thing. This is expressed by Kafka's fear to be united with his own shadow, which is what happens when you eventually 'fall'. At the same moment, Nakata is pushed to stop searching for lost cats (with which he, at the start of the novel, makes some extra money) and start a search for the other half of his shadow (which can only be found in the light).

Murakami keeps on singing the same old Japanese song: 'the brushwood we gather – stack it together, it makes a hut; pull it apart, a field once more' (in Tanizaki, 46).

Let me give an example of how these earthly processes of figuring, as I called it, enact what we might call one event central to *Kafka on the Shore*: the death of Johnny Walker. Johnny Walker performs vivisection on cats. After quite a long journey in which Nakata is lured into the darkest and the most obscure backstreets of the city, Walker confronts Nakata (the cat) with his gruesome slicing open of cats and the eating of their hearts. Walker then demands Nakata to kill him, as this is the only way he can be stopped. Nakata knives him two times, after saying, 'I don't feel like myself' ([2002] 2005, 136). Covered in blood, Nakata falls asleep, but when he wakes up, the blood is gone. The blood seems, however, to have continued its journey, for at the same time, Kafka, in the city of Takamatsu, awakens for no apparent reason drenched in blood ([Murakami [2002] 2005, 64–5). Later in the book, blood again continues its flow, not bothered by being either on the inside or on the outside of the human body, when Kafka concludes: 'I spread my fingers apart and stare at the palms of both hands, looking for bloodstains. There aren't any. No scent of blood, no stiffness. The blood must have already, in its own silent way, seeped inside' ([Murakami [2002] 2005, 210).

Murakami not so much shows us where the blood is, but how and where the blood *matters*. For although the undercurrent may be personified with Nakata, it is not 'limited' to its persona, in any way; it cracks through the narrative as a whole. The undercurrent gives form to the abstract life of Kafka/Nakata, as it gives life to Colonel Sanders, Johnny Walker, all the cats, all the allies and all the blood between them. Kafka, the modernist, the Cartesian, the one in search for logic, is in fear of it. It is this fear that Nishitani (inspired by Buddhism and Heidegger) warns us against the most: this self-centred or logos-centred dogma of a modernism that fears the unforeseen, that fears another earth. Only when moving towards what he calls an 'absolute nothingness', this anotherness can be met and felt to the fullest: 'Everything is now truly empty, and this means that all things make themselves present here and now, just as they are, in their original reality. They present themselves in their suchness, their tathatā. This is non-attachment' (Nishitani 1982, 34). Only when moving towards the naiveté of Nakata, rejecting Kafka, the presumed hero of the story who lives in fear, this anotherness can be met and felt to the fullest.

Then, whereas the metaphysical spaces in which Kafka happens reveal the plot of the book (its humanist and timely realities), the pragmatic inhuman spaces of Nakata *crack them open*. Nakata, the cat, has no idea what is about to happen, but he does not fear it. He doesn't know what will happen and what has happened. That is why Nakata never feels 'like himself' as he so often tells us. He feels space, the city, the environment. He feels that the blood is coming. He is confident that in the end he will find the important thing on the right place. Somehow. Nakata is the unforeseen. In the chapters he figures, this constantly takes place. For instance, the truck driver Hoshina, normally confined by his usual routes and orders from above, through Nakata, enters into new spaces, new environments and is not fearful but inspired by the new spaces to come. By turning the stone, the spectres meet the spirit as Nakata immanently produces the magic formula; *that what is interior is also exterior.* A 'clopen' set in motion.

It has been very difficult, in the age of the (Cartesian) Bright Idea, to understand the Shadow as a power in itself, independent of the light. Heidegger, especially in his later works (on technology, on art), made an effort to undo the dark of the spell of the light, showing us that everywhere one sees a shadow that 'is a manifest, though impenetrable, testimony to the concealed emitting of light' (1977, 154). But perhaps it was only Gaston Bachelard who understood that we should read more poetry to understand how we frightened souls prefer to say close to the light but are always already enclosed by an objectless night. In the cellar, in the attic, in the limitless Great Outside; *everywhere darkness awaits us.*

Poets like Rilke, but also photographers like Antoni Arissa Asmarats, start from the shade, allowing light only to be the absence of the shade. But still these are rare cases. Tanizaki is right when he concludes:

> And so it has come to be that the beauty of a Japanese room depends on a variation of shadows, heavy shadows against light shadows – it has nothing else. Westerners are amazed at the simplicity of Japanese rooms, perceiving in them no more than ashen walls bereft of ornament. Their reaction is understandable, but it betrays a failure to comprehend the mystery of shadows.
>
> ([1933] 2001, 29)

The lacquerware, the gold, the darkness of the inner rooms: Tanizaki keeps stressing the power of the dark and the way in which the light is so often used to identify (subject and object) and to dispel the shadows in the furthest corners, something which runs against the basic experience of Japanese space. Light is the territorializing force that our modern hero, Kafka, is so attracted to. Of course, it is with Nakata that the true liberation of the dark takes place. For Nakata, the cat that crawls, that touches the earth with its stomach, that desires to feel the power of the dark matter, feels the ethics it includes. Nakata feels that it is not light that creates life (organic and an-organic and non-organic) but that it is in the earth that powers come to being.

All forms evolve only from the dark. Not from isolation but from connection. Shades merge and split, drawing shadows in shadows that function as one, undercurrents that persevere in their being.

The cracks of the contemporary

Michel Serres has told us over and over again that the difference between fiction and non-fiction is a very recent invention of academia. It must, therefore, be essentially modernist too. Starting from the idea that the truth is out there (and not in the Book), academic writings are considered closer to this truth than the so-called books of fiction that artists produce. All of these explicit and implicit oppositions, definitions, suspicions are, of course, highly questionable, to say the least. From a Spinozist perspective, these claims to truth make absolutely no sense at all. When we read the works of Murakami, when we map the processes of figuring as they guide us through the book, the freedom proposed to us readers is no different from the freedom that springs from the works of Deleuze and Guattari and from the work of Serres. In Murakami's *1Q84* and *Kafka on the Shore*, as well as in Michel Tournier's *Friday*, we read how the unreal intervenes in the real. Real and unreal are part of a single flow and in that flow new landscapes are explored: they produce art and they think geophilosophy.

The abovementioned books by Murakami and Tournier realize many different interventions in the religious, humanist and capitalist entanglements that make up the present. They, consequently, are able to offer us a wholly different earth which we had been blind to – an earth that we for some reason were unable to think before. Let us start with the most unreal moment that actually binds two of these books together.

Both in Tournier's *Friday* as in Murakami's *1Q84*, the dying of the great goat is the advent of something new, unforeseen. In both books, a goat [Pan?] functions as a sort of a sacrifice, becoming the medium through which another earth is invited to realize itself. This new and unknown earth has no relation whatsoever to the earth as we know it. In *1Q84* it presents itself in the opening of the chrysalis. In *Friday* it is the opening of the beach. In both books, this is actually the grand theme: the smoothest of all surfaces *is about to crack*.

When I talk of 'another earth' here, I mean the earth in the most material sense of the word as well as the ideas that follow from it. And when I say that the earth is unforeseen, I mean that our thinking falls short, for whatever reason, to understand this earth. I completely agree here with Michel Serres when he offers us the recipe of modern Western thinking:

Take away the world around the battles, keep only conflicts and debates, thick with humanity and purified of things, and you obtain stage theatre, most of our narratives and philosophies, history, and all of social science: the interesting spectacle they call cultural? Does anyone ever say where the master and the slave fight it out? Our culture abhors the world.

([1990] 1995: 3)

Let us get back to our books – to the crack as it announces itself when Robinson realizes that he is unable to live the life that the deserted island is offering him and when Aomame, the main character of *1Q84*, realizes that the city of Tokyo is not the city of Tokyo as she knew it before. That moment I call the crack. It's the moment that marks both books. Both books happen at this crack.

As readers, our aim is not so much to follow the words from page to page. Rather, we feel the infinitesimal cracks slowly, but meticulously mapping the weakest parts of the old earth's surface. The earth we believed to live on, the organized, territorialized earth, while we read the book, gently breaks open, cracking the hard surface, presenting us the softness within. The chrysalis, the pop, is smooth, is infinite and has an ideal form when it comes to resisting the pressures from both inside and outside. But the powers that have been hidden inside, powers that have been hidden for us, are now slowly, but steadily, surfacing. And, of course, this is what we fear. For we all know that something is about to happen that will destroy everything as we now know it.

We know very well that the crack does not stop with the pop or with the borders of the city, with the beach or with the island. When we live through the book, as weeks pass by, we feel that because of this crack, both Robinson and Aomame have been cracked, lacerated and laid open. The entire island of Speranza as well as the city of Tokyo, as they include flora and fauna that live it, the languages that live, the organs that make up the biospheres that live it – nothing was left untouched by the crack.

Already on the first pages of the books, both Robinson and Aomame have entered another world, a world that is in no way the same as the world we once knew. The crack has always already happened long before we notice. Robinson and Aomame will try to find out how they are cracked and how the deserted island and the city of Tokyo are cracked. What caused it? Robinson asks us: Why is this deserted island not functioning like the inhabited world that I lived before? Why are its most elementary systems of religion and capitalism not working here? What is this wholly other life, which I am suddenly subjected to, all about? Aomame wonders: What kind of city is this, this dark and obscure non-place run by the Little People that never care to reveal themselves (except through the goats' mouth)? I cannot sense this city and only feel a fear revealing itself in this wholly other soft pulse. This new and unknown Tokyo is a city that oozes out, whose heartbeat is a wave. It is a city that exists only in and through its liquid rhythm, which I cannot dance to.

We (Robinson and Aomame) have no idea what the future will bring us. Death, for sure. But in what way? Since this death it brings us is ungraspable (again, nonsensical), we are dying to know what comes after. Lucretius told us that everything will reappear but in another form, a form that bears no resemblance to those forms we are acquainted with. New forms will be formed. New biospheres will be formed. Should we make notes; should we use little stones or breadcrumbs to ensure the minimal of continuity possible? Should we try to hang on to some sort of linearity, some sort of cause and effect?

There is a crack in the world, as Nakata had already noticed. There is a crack in the world. Aomame, in *1Q84*, cannot cope with the changing world, is overtaken by fear and searches for ways to escape this new earth. In *Kafka on the Shore*, the other main character,

Kafka or the boy named crow, has a similar response, insisting on continuing his life as much as possible. Stuck to the territories they are accustomed to, to the grammar they have always used, the signs and images that they are familiar with, Kafka and Aomame live a reality that is as real as those stars that we see in the sky every evening. Stars that have been gone for thousands of years already. There is a crack in the world, Nakata notices time and again

How is Nakata aware of that? And how is it that Robinson too, all of a sudden, sees 'another island' beyond the present one? In *Kafka on the Shore*, from the start of the book, Nakata is wholly different from Kafka. Kafka is a pretty young man, rational, whose world all of a sudden seems to fall apart. Nakata is not rational at all. At least not in Kafka's sense. Nakata is a strange character: talking the language of cats but not really of man, moving in ways considered impossible for man too and, at night, popping up in the strangest places. Nakata, in many ways, is 'not-human'. Unhuman even. Perhaps because of that, he is extremely sensitive to what is going on: extremely sensitive, able to feel the earth in ways unknown to many of us. He is away experimenting with different forms of language as a means to explore the unknown earth, to feel what forms of life this unknown earth allows for. Kafka is the traditional hero of the story, a tragic figure who desperately seeks for ways to expand an idea of normality that might have worked before but that has nothing to do with the world in which he lives now. He is afraid that he, that his world, that everything, will die. Which has – of course – already happened. Long ago.

Robinson, in Tournier's *Friday*, has the stubbornness (the rationale, the fear) of Kafka but finds out, the hard way, that he has to live the life that Speranza, the island, wants him to live. Living the deserted island, he has to explore the unknown earth; he has to feel what forms of life the island allows. And Robinson actually succeeds to live in this world without Others, in this unterritorialized world in which thinking and the earth have once again merged. Where the earth, in all of its appearances, is once again the object of thinking while thinking is the idea of the earth. Where 'thinking' and 'earth' are actually the same thing.

Aomame, Kafka, Robinson and Nakata offer us an aesthetics, which is a philosophy of nature, and my claim is that they do that most convincingly in their practicing of time. Let me come back to a few concepts of time introduced earlier in the book, which is very useful for analysing what is at stake here. First of all, there is the present, which fills time completely with Aomame and Kafka. Past and future for them are relative to the present, consequences of the religious, humanist and capitalist reality of the day. Aomame and Kafka are firmly woven into the present which is why they are in fear of the cracks in the earth underneath them as they are afraid of their wounds. For them the present absorbs everything, as they are absorbed by the present. There is no way out. For them the present territorializes the earth, measures the earth, fixes it and intends to realize it according to its standards. Time, with Aomame and Kafka, is the gradual movement from present to present, from the slow and organized shifts in the religious, humanist and capitalist realities of the day. Yet always too fast. Very dangerous.

Robinson (after the crack, in the second half of the book) and Nakata, however, live a different time. A smoother time, unquantifiable, which actually lacks a present. They live a world in which the religious, humanist and capitalist reality of the day does not matter (anymore).

Their time knows of a virtual past and a virtual future. But this past and future do not have a relation to each other; they do not wait for a relation; they are in every way free floating, unformed. Robinson and Nakata have found an immense freedom as their lives are not confined into a present and the limits that it flows into (its past, its future). Robinson and Nakata, with smiles on their faces, ward off any realization of a present, using the virtual past and the virtual future as their tools to intervene in anything that even remotely resembles a present. They never stop playing with the religious, humanist and capitalist realities that they find on their way. For them, time is what needs to find ways to disturb the present and to deterritorialize it. Full of all sorts of difficulties, they live a life filled with joy, very much in contrast to Aomame and Kafka.

For Robinson and Nakata, the present is nothing but the permanent crisis that is open to an infinite series of interventions. It is a crisis that they understand only through its cracks and what these cracks can do. They play the desires (or forces) of the cracks, map how it breaks open the surfaces and speculate upon this new past and this new future presented. Time, for Robinson and Nakata does not 'exist', but has to be invented over and over again. (This also explains why both of them do not age: they were not young and they will never turn old.) Their time is a *pure and empty* form of time; their time comes down to the eternal truth of time, that does not allow itself to be measured. Their time is permanently changing, as it traverses, without limits, the crisis of today. Being empty, these times, in fact, coincide with the cracks that mark the contemporary. *They are the same thing.* As said, the cracks are not so much 'in' time, as they happen with the time (I see them in the con-temporary): the cracks that disturb the religious, humanist and capitalist realities of today and that keep on disturbing these realities (as indeed this form of time knows no present). The cracks keep on playing (with) the present.

In Tournier's *Friday* and in Murakami's *Kafka on the Shore*, Robinson and Nakata, respectively, personify this second form of time, this intervening qualitative force which we could also refer to as 'the creative act'. It is their virtual presence (of Robinson and Nakata) that smoothens these books, not just from cover to cover but in making all sorts of transversal connections to *all that is outside of it*. Robinson and Nakata intervene in every crisis they somehow end up in, thereby cracking the hegemonies of the present. Here comes the good news. Robinson is not stuck on some remote place in the Pacific; he actually lives on *your* deserted island and he shows you another island if you are willing to see it. Nakata crawls the backstreets of *your* city, he is talking to *your* cats and he protects *your* darkness. Again, how different they are from Aomame and Kafka, whose lives are by all means locked up in the book! Too attached to the 'worlds of others' (which is another way of verbalizing the religious, humanist and capitalist relations they find themselves in), they remind us of Pierre Dumaine and Ève Charlier, in Jean-Paul Sartre's *The Chips Are Down* ([1947] 1948), of whom we know, from the very start of the book, that they are doomed. Their lives are already over before the stories unfold – stories in which nothing happens, as Pierre and Ève *do not live, but fear* the cracks of the contemporary. The same goes for Aomame and Kafka. Their lives don't matter.

There are many things happening with Robinson and Nakata, many accidents that do not just hit them but that, from the very start of the two books, realize wholly other worlds. The strange accident that befell Nakata in the newsflash at the start of *Kafka on the Shore* and the shipwrecking that befell Robinson at the start of *Friday* are immediately tearing us away from the present and only function as the starting points for the series of accidents that are about to follow. Robinson and Nakata became the men of their misfortunes, but as they did that so well (so beautifully), they must both have led a very happy life (to paraphrase Goethe). They became worthy of what happened to them, worthy of their accidents, worthy of the wounds they embodied. Having dealt with their accidents so marvellously, they both discovered a new life, a new body and, consequently, a new earth.

The creative act happens with time, yet it is necessarily useless to the present. What happened to Robinson and Nakata, for that matter, was completely irrelevant to the present. It made no sense, at all. Let us be very rigorous about this; the creative act cannot play a role in the religious, humanist and capitalist realities of the day. The creative act is, however, extremely valuable to the contemporary, as it keeps on fighting the illusions of the present, narratives like capitalism and organized religion, like state power and identity. The creative act will always traverse all of these fables with a single blow, breaking them open immanently.

The creative act simply does not function with its strategies which aim at securing binary oppositions, securing hierarchies and securing the ongoing internalizations of these hierarchies in place. There are many people that, for that reason, do not want the creative act to happen – that consider Nakata a crazy person and Robinson a savage (a villain, an outsider). There are many people that feel the need (the fear?) to defend the strategies of the present – all the people in power, for instance, as they feel that their lives depend on it. And, of course, they will do everything to stay in power, to persevere in their (zombified) being, to stay in the present. But it is not just the masters who depend on the present but also the slaves who fight for their slavery are trapped by it. Aomame and Kafka, as they both feel very much hurt by the creative act, by the disturbances of the reality of the day, by the cracks in the contemporary, actively choose to fight this wholly other earth that they are confronted with. Because of the fear of the unknown, because of ignorance, because of loyalty, because of all sorts of 'prisoner's dilemmas', they rather reject these cracks and deny their own wounds, or will even try to 'fix' them (which is impossible), in a final attempt to continue their lives into a non-existing reality. Their lives are like stars that can be seen in the dark sky, but that have died out a long time ago.

So, what can we conclude about this second form of time? What can we say about these disturbing powers, these cracks in the contemporary, these creative acts? First of all, it should be said that they are realized in a single stroke. Yet by two means. *They exist in geophilosophy, while they only conclude with the artwork.* Or to phrase this in broader terms: they only happen in thought while they produce the creative. This also means that neither geophilosophy nor art functions in the present. Geophilosophy and art are, in themselves, not taken up into the religious, humanist and capitalist reality of the day. Yet they have a very important role in the contemporary as geophilosophy and art, together, have the power to crack it. They have the weight of the entire earth at their disposal, to put the realities of the present under pressure, cracking them where they are most vulnerable, where the surfaces that aim to keep them intact are most fragile.

And thus, thinking from the cracks of the contemporary, (per) forming the cracks that intervene in the present, in the end, is not at all limited to aesthetics and epistemology. On the contrary, through posthumanism, new materialism, ecofeminism, but also through quantum mechanics and so many explorations in (practice-based artistic) research, the cracks are lived. Starting from the cracks of the contemporary, we experience how all the crises that mark the twenty-first century are connected and that the minor fissures of one crisis lead us to the major cracks of the next: from capitalism to the nation state, digitalization to Corona, from climate change to mass extinction to overconsumption to the militarization of police.

Staying with the trouble, as Donna Haraway calls it, geophilosophy and the arts are jointly in search for new forms to live in this earth. Through new alliances, we organize; we take up responsibility. With Robinson and Nakata, we imagine a world otherwise; we intervene in the religious, humanist and capitalist crises.

We start thinking from the crack, as it is the crack that matters.

The wound (I was born to embody)

Every heart is broken! Near the end of his novel *Colorless Tsukuru Tazaki and His Years of Pilgrimage*, Haruki Murakami concludes ([2013] 2015, 259) that it is the wound which essentially precedes all the different forms of harmony marking Tsukuru's life.

> One heart is not connected to another through harmony alone. They are, instead, linked deeply through their wounds. Pain linked to pain, fragility to fragility. There is no silence without a cry of grief, no forgiveness without bloodshed, no acceptance without a passage through acute loss. That is what lies at the root of true harmony.

Murakami comes towards us with two vital theses in this paragraph. The first thesis wards off the anthropocentrism (humanism) that is often (implicitly) presupposed when one thinks the wound. Wounds are not to be considered one's own deficiencies; they are no minor failures of nature that happen to somebody by accident and there is nothing personal about them. Consequently, the wound is never a part of me, nor of anyone or anything else. The emptiness of the wound cracks itself through a series of bodies, making the wound always a shared wound; it leads a singular existence and realizes itself in different ways upon the surfaces of life. What happens is that I come to embody the wound, just as you do, just as so many others do. The wound is in the non-organic, the organic *and* the inorganic as it cuts through everything. It cuts through the microbe as through a galaxy, an ice crystal and a pack of wolves. And yes, if it cuts in the same way through you as it cuts through me, then we might find a common way to ease each other's pain. We might love each other. Be together. Function as one.

The question is not whether a wound can heal. The wound is eternal and endless, as it knows no beginning or end. When Tsukuru claims that he wants to put things behind him – meaning slowly closing the wound and conquering the pain – this has nothing to do with healing. The rest of the book confirms this: the wound will always be there. As Sara, another character in the novel, puts it: 'I understand, but maybe it only appears, from the outside, that the wound is closed' (idem, 88). Later, Tsukuru also acknowledges this: 'Sixteen years have gone by, but it feels like the wound is still there inside me. Like it's still bleeding. Something happened recently, something very significant to me, that made me realize this' (idem, 137).

Sara and Tsukuru are perfectly right; wounds cannot heal. They will always accompany us. This does not mean that 'we' are always 'wounded' in the sense that we live our lives in a continuous imperfect state. Life has already taught us, in many ways, that sickness does not exclude health and vice versa. There are always a thousand tiny sicknesses and a thousand tiny healths at work. Sometimes health takes over, other times sickness. But neither one disappears. They transform, mutate, undergo a radical metamorphosis. This is similar in the case of wounds. They accompany us, but will never be our companion; we don't choose them; we don't invite them or say goodbye. Wounds surface, cause pain, disappear unnoticed and come back when they decide. Gao Xingjiang ([1990] 2001) shows us beautifully how this works in his novel *Soul Mountain*, which talks about a long journey through the Sichuan mountains that follows a (false?) diagnosis of lung cancer. The diagnosis is a mis/fortune that is at work in all the events to follow. Walking from village to village, the main character, only referred to as 'I', is often accompanied by wounds. And so are 'you' and 'she', other returning characters in the book.

Wounds are visible in one situation and invisible in the other, leaving the main character (whoever this might be) by themselves again. Wounds accompany 'I', as they accompany the landscape being travelled, surrounding 'I' as part of the real and unreal swarm. The wound follows from the swarm of little deaths that roams the lands of Sichuan, giving rise to everything that happens during his journey. The traditions that the landscapes house, as well as the mountains, the gorges, the woods, the lakes; in the wounds, all of them meet, accompany one another and start a myriad of love affairs. At the heart of these events, wounds transform, mould into other wounds, merge into bigger ones or shred into pieces. Wounds surface and disappear again. But they will always roll along. They continue to matter.

Most human beings, Seneca already noticed, complain about the meanness of nature. Many feel as if the Others wound them, hurt them so intensely, that they are unable to pick up their lives again, that they no longer feel 'human'. Catherine Malabou analyses this when conceptualizing 'the new wounded', as she calls it. Analysing the 'new age of political violence' ([2007] 2012, 156) or the effects of alcoholism and abuse (in the case of Marguerite Duras in *The Ontology of the Accident* [2009] 2012), she stresses that the plasticity of the brain is regressing, that the brain is sometimes unable to cope with these severe traumas and injuries. And that's when death occurs while life still goes on. That's when the traumatized become the zombified; they just don't care; nothing matters to them anymore. And this then refers not only to the terrorists of our age but also to artists like Duras and to all of our contemporaries whose lives have cracked, as Malabou claims.

I should be very precise with this. I agree with Seneca, with the fact that we always already no longer feel human. But in contrast to Malabou, I refuse to follow the negative (Hegelian) reading of the wound and instead adopt the Stoic and Spinozist perspective, which goes completely the other way. This time, the wound is not secondary (it doesn't happen to me) but primary (it was always already there). This time, the wound is not that which endangers life; *it is the wound that makes life worth living.*

It is the wound that forces us to strive for the good (Eudamonia). Wounds will never heal; problems will not be solved. I agree with Maurice Blanchot on this: 'What is prime is not the fullness of being; what is prime is the crack and the fissure, erosion and destruction, intermittence and gnawing privation' ([1959] 2003, 38). For him, it is in the work of Antonin Artaud that this nothingness is most obviously at work: 'It is a pressure that is so terrible that it expresses him, while at the same time demanding that he devote himself completely to producing it and maintaining its expression' (idem).

Life, then, is not nothingness, Blanchot shows us; it is the invention which follows, which we call 'a life'. This is also what Murakami is expressing all the time. In other words, life is a struggle that is driven by a longing for death. It is not an inclination for death. It is a response to the nothingness to which it succumbs. Life is therefore always a will to be reborn, to realize one's non-carnal birth on the emptiness of the wounds it sees itself confronted with. But also, human life is 'one long goodbye', as the T'ang Dynasty poet Yu Wuling and Murakami's Johnny Walker have already told us. The questions I therefore propose are: How do we live the wound? How do we live the many wounds that crack the surfaces we embody? And how do we cope with the actual and virtual undercurrents upon which we weave our everyday lives?

Murakami's second thesis concerns time. Just as the wound does not happen to anyone, it also does not happen in time. In other words, the wound is never present. It does not take place, it is not embedded in the different realities that make up the present, and yet, it is always already here. Eri, Tsukuru's high school friend, confirms this near the end of the novel when she states that the wound happens 'in all the echoes that surround us, in the light, in shapes, in every single...' ([2013] 2015, 259). How well put: it doesn't happen in the present, in the presence of the body, as part of the relations being established in what counts as the here and now.

The wound lies at the heart; it is the cause, of all of its events.

Being not-present means the existence of the wound cannot and will not take part in the religious, humanist and capitalist realities of the day. As mentioned earlier, the wound does not 'function with' anything. The wound is untouchable and will always find a way to escape from these realities. Hidden under weak and fragile surfaces, which will remain super sensitive and ready to crack again, the wound remains. It itches. It pulls. It's not just a scar that is more sensitive to bad weather compared to the rest of your skin. The wound is open to all the affects that surround it. As the cracking never stops, the wound always already has a wholly other life of itself and it will search for other ways of cracking and other forms of existing, ad infinitum.

The present is made up of harmonies and melodies, of connections and relations. But the wound immanently acts through its virtual impact on the present. Brushing up against the present, feeling the present (stroking it, rubbing it), the resonances and vibrations caused by its sharpness and grain put maximum tension on the thinnest of the surfaces, and thus the wound acts, intervenes and cracks the times. The wound, in that sense, *happens with* the present. And as such it introduces the present to the contemporary – the wide range of possible and impossible acts that mark our days that comes with time but is not restricted to it and that actually invites us to open ourselves up to the power of all of those undercurrents that we have been blind to.

Unrelated to the present, not knowing the present even, the wound should be considered the power that causes the present to crack and thereby opening it up to the contemporary. But does this not mean that both the past and the future, in effect, happen only at the moment the wound intervenes? Can we not conclude from this that the past and the future, therefore, only take place on the wound? The past and the future are two very different elements in time that might appear to be linked to the present but that in no way can be placed in a linear sequence with it (which is obviously a humanist delusion). They happen together on the emptiness of the wound. In fact, they can only take place on it. Only the emptiness of the wound matters. Time offers us a chaosmosis of pasts and futures, but it is only upon the emptiness of the wound where past and future meet and function as one.

The wound lures us in. It lies deep inside us and lies deep inside everything and everyone else, inviting us into the void. It is the black (the colourless) nothingness that contains everything and nothing. The religious, humanist and capitalist realities make up the present, a surface upon which everything occurs, but the wound within gives it its life. Joë Bousquet is perhaps most convincing in showing us how the overcoming of the wound is actually the key to life: 'Become the man of your misfortunes; learn to embody their perfection and brilliance' (in Deleuze [1969] 1990, 149).

Rethinking subjectivity, Sigmund Freud, in his *Introduction to Psychoanalysis*, gave us a sharp analysis of the three narcissistic wounds that mark humanity in its essence, while cracking their way into every possible direction and dimension to come. Three wounds that open up voids in our mental, social and environmental ecologies (Freud [1917] 2012). All three, in their togetherness, crack the humanist myth, a stubborn fantasy of exceptionalism, which, in the first place, aims to secure the human's 'special position' on earth. Anthropocentrism was, of course, not invented by René Descartes but was always the way to justify to the creation of difference, the turning of difference into hierarchy and finally the organization and institutionalization of this hierarchy, putting the 'I think' (the cogito) on top.

This humanist myth is cracked three times. Firstly, Freud notes the realization that our earth is not the centre of the universe, an insight ascribed to Copernicus. Secondly, he refers to the findings of biological research at the time (specifically Charles Darwin and Alfred Russel Wallace), which show that man was never radically different from the other species in the animal kingdom. Finally and rightfully so, Freud mentions his own research, noting that the importance of the unconscious to human thought puts a big question mark on humankind's supposed rationality.

Freud emphasized that none of these three ideas should be considered 'discoveries' to be attributed to particular wise men in the history of Western thought. Freud was never interested in setting up epistemologies, philosophies of science or histories of thought, for that matter. Freud, the psychoanalyst, was working on case studies; he was interested in the *production* of human subjectivity. He was interested in *how individuals live their wounds*, what it means to live one's misfortunes, what it means to be worthy of one's time, to 'feel' the misfortunes in which one finds oneself and how this happens irrespective of time and space. In short: these wounds have not been done to us since the idle belief of nineteenth-century humanism obscured our thinking and our relation to the world. These are the wounds of humankind (have always been and always will be).

Freud stressed that the ideas of Copernicus, for example, could already be found in the Alexandrian doctrines. Following the German physiologist Emil du Bois-Reymond, a Berlin-based theorist writing in the mid-nineteenth century and a major influence on Freud, the American philosopher William James and many voices in early psychoanalysis, Freud stresses how closely related these three wounds are. He notes, for instance, how in a eulogy to Darwin written in 1882, du Bois-Reymond claimed 'Darwin seems to me to be the Copernicus of the organic world' (du Bois-Reymond 1883, 249). Even more interesting: because he doesn't seem to recognize the wounds of his era, du Bois-Reymond critiques Descartes for not being worthy of the times in which he lived. Descartes knew about Giordano Bruno, who indeed lived his misfortunes. Bruno was well known for his thoughts about pantheism and his rejection of a centre (of the universe, of the self) and wrote, with admirable honesty, about how he dealt with the theological and scientific crisis that hit him during his lifetime. His ideas and beliefs then famously led to his execution.

Descartes, instead, chose to do philosophy and mathematics in a Machiavellian style. He was highly interested in the centres of power (the cogito, the origin of the coordinate system $(0,0)$) and what this meant in the present-day religious, humanist and capitalist realities that dominated his day and age. I mentioned this at the start of this book: Antonio Negri is right when he considers Descartes' *Discourse de la Methode* to be 'the bildungsroman of the bourgeois' (Negri 1970). And even Voetius (see Serrurier 1930, 102), the seventeenth-century theologian, was right: what an arrogance to place the human being above everything else!

Descartes did not seem to live his wounds, as he had no interest in the undercurrents that cracked the realities he wanted to control. Descartes was very different from his predecessor Bruno and also from his contemporary Spinoza, who preferred not to live the realities of the day altogether. Spinoza lived the careful life of the heretic (also knowing what happened to Bruno) and wrote the *Ethics* practically in solitude (only a few of his closest friends had read the manuscript before his death), the book that has the power to change every day and age.

When Freud noted three wounds that crack humanism, he told us something about what the task of philosophy should be: philosophy (or the humanities in general even) should feel the wounds that are buried deep inside of us that will never heal and that continue to crack the world. Philosophers are not doctors; their calling is not to heal the wound. They spend their life searching for ways to live the wound – indeed, to be worthy of the wounds, the cracks and all the undercurrents that matter in our times. And, of course, as we are willing to open our eyes (our senses), we can always find more wounds that accompany us, easily. When Roland Barthes says, he is interested in language because it wounds or seduces him, is he not asking us whether our relation to language is yet another one of those deep carnal wounds that demand from us to live a creative life? I'm sure this is where the philosophers and writers of fiction that feature in this book fully agree: Deleuze, Haraway, Bousquet, Murakami all live this wound beautifully.

The shared force of geophilosophy and the arts is to find ways to live the wounds that matter today, which does not mean that artists and geophilosophers should search for ways to identify these wounds. Being bothered by them, being constantly reminded of them, being in pain because of these wounds (limping, catching a breath), it means that you experiment with a creativity that is always in the process of mapping these wounds. The goal is not to write about them, to consider the wounds as entities opposite of you (as objects), give form to them and analyse them as such. On the contrary, there is *only the necessity to live the void that they are.*

Making art and doing geophilosophy only happen because of a sensitivity for the wounds that cut deep through our human and not-so-human selves. The three wounds of Freud, the wound of language that Barthes distinguishes, but, of course, all of the crises of the contemporary, all of the cracks as they groove the surface of the earth today, are lived intensely in art and in geophilosophy. The true artist and the true geophilosopher cannot live easy lives. Yayoi Kusama and Antonin Artaud are not the exception but rather set the standard. All too often, they can hardly bear the misfortunes that crack them open, that threaten them in such a way that they can only write, act and perform, in order to resist. It is not a choice to live a life like this. And there is definitely nothing 'romantic' about it. It is a necessity.

Addressing these wounds in one's writings, one's artworks and one's life can best be seen as an ongoing negotiation, between life and non-life, death and non-death. The non-humanist and untimely ideas of the wound *have* to be occupied with unease and discomfort. It is too easy for the artist and the geophilosopher to be anti-fascist in a post-media age where the algorithms of Facebook give rise to many seemingly new forms of narcissism, that, as always, capture us in the economic, social and political dreams of the Strong Leader and of the Fascist Rule that we see on the rise today. It is too easy just to oppose, to reject, to *critique* any crisis that befalls us. We have to open ourselves up to it, to recognize in what way this crisis was always already a part of us and to take up responsibility for it.

Deleuze and Guattari already stressed that you have to see the fascist inside you, the fascist you yourself sustain, nourish and cherish ([1980] 1987, 215). This fascist is both personal and collective; it is at work in every part of our daily life and cuts through the state, neighbourhood relations and the pollution of Lake Erie. The genealogies of these fascist machineries change but do not stop realizing themselves in unexpected forms of reality. Being responsible now has little to do with standing up for the weak and the powerless and taking a position. On the contrary, to live the wound, one has to escape every present; one has to start living the void, the crack itself. Map the microfascisms at work!

In his introduction to Deleuze and Guattari's *Anti-Oedipus*, Michel Foucault praised the authors by saying that this new form of thinking they delivered was not some sort of flashy Hegel. It was an introduction to the non-fascist life (see Deleuze and Guattari [1972] 1984 and also Dolphijn and Braidotti 2021). After geophilosophy, but also after art, Deleuze and Guattari lived the wound of 1968, exploring its void, the mighty crack that it opened up in French academia, in the Parisian intelligentsia, in Vincennes' woods, in red wine, in antipsychiatry, in thought. In a similar vein, Michel Serres is living the wound of 1945, the wound created by Little Boy as it was dropped on Hiroshima, on science, on Nature. Deleuze, Guattari and Serres lived their wounds; they embodied its perfection and brilliance. They found their freedom, which was solid and complete (I wrote extensively on this in Dolphijn 2018).

In the final stages of Murakami's novel, Tsukuru finds a way to live his freedom too, finds a way to live his freedom in his non-carnal birth.

He calmed himself, shut his eyes, and fell asleep. The rear light of consciousness, like the last express train of the night, began to fade into the distance, gradually speeding up, growing smaller until it was, finally, sucked into the depths of the night, where it disappeared. All that remained was the sound of the wind slipping through a stand of white birch trees.

Isn't this pure life, the immanence of immanence? In his last text, Deleuze talked of 'a life' as a complete power, a complete bliss, concluding: 'it is an absolute immediate consciousness whose very activity no longer refers to a being that is ceaselessly posed in life' (2001, 27). It is the wound which is incarnated but is a pure virtuality itself. Freed from the passions, he remained in sense, as breath, in the theme that runs throughout the book, the pure power that is mobile and precise. Free from the present. Invisible. Right on the wound where life takes place.

Part 4

GEOMETER, SHOW ME A NEW EARTH

We need the geometer to actually do their job, which is; to start from the crises of the contemporary, to imagine the earth and the forms of life that belong to it. More than in previous parts of the book, the final part of my meditation introduces us to a series of contemporary thinkers and makers. Here, the geometer takes us to the new land of materialist inquiry: from how quantum mechanics emphasizes that it is the relation that matters and how architects and choreographers think about 'the angle', to how feminist thought and pagan rituals propose us earthly environments that inhabit the contemporary.

In the end, I will return to the importance of imagination with which I started this book. With the help of Murakami and with all of the creative writers (inside and outside of academia) that accompanied the geometer in their search, the geometer shows us that the real/unreal, or the truth for that matter, *only* happens in thought and is produced in the work of art. And there is nothing human about this. It takes place on the crack, the earthly crack.

IMAGE 4.
Credit: Fragment from *Leak*, © Oscar Chan Yik Long

The geometer starts from a physics beyond critique

In an interview with Karen Barad undertaken by Iris van der Tuin and myself, the mention of the word 'critique', as part of an extensive question that had little to do with this concept, caused her to make a strong statement *against* the status of critical thinking, as a residue of Cartesianism, in the humanities today:

> I am not interested in critique. In my opinion, critique is over-rated, over-emphasized, and over-utilized, to the detriment of feminism. As Bruno Latour signals in an article entitled 'Why has Critique Run out of Steam? From Matters of Fact to Matters of Concern' (2004), critique is a tool that keeps getting used out of habit perhaps, but it is no longer the tool needed for the kinds of situations we now face. Critique has been the tool of choice for so long, and our students find themselves so well trained in critique that they can spit out a critique with the push of a button. Critique is too easy, especially when a commitment to reading with care

no longer seems to be a fundamental element of critique. So as I explain to my students, reading and writing are ethical practices, and critique misses the mark. Now, I understand that there is a different valence to the notion of critique in Europe than there is in the United States; nonetheless, I think this point is important. Critique is all too often not a deconstructive practice, that is, a practice of reading for the constitutive exclusions of those ideas we cannot do without, but a destructive practice meant to dismiss, to turn aside, to put someone or something down– another scholar, another feminist, a discipline, an approach, et cetera.

(Barad in Dolphijn and van der Tuin, 49)

Barad continues the argument by elaborating on this distinction between a critique that is deconstructive and one that is destructive, noting that the latter strategy (of dismissing, turning aside and/or putting someone or something down) particularly bothers her. The former, the deconstructive critique, this 'practice of reading for the constitutive exclusions of those ideas we cannot do without', seems to come much closer to her scholarly practice.

The difference between a deconstructive and a destructive critique first of all concerns ethics. It comes down to saying that, as a scholar, it is all too easy to place oneself 'outside' of a tradition, to restrain oneself from involvement in the matters at stake. In feminist theory, this engagement with the contemporary is of importance especially after Donna Haraway. Haraway's (1988) emphasis on situated knowledges is not aimed at identifying *a* woman's way of knowing (prominent in feminist thinking since 1968) but rather aims at mapping *a multiplicity* of women's ways of knowing, an unlimited and undefined (not beginning with subjectivity or femininity, or by any a priori category) search for alternative perspectives. Instead of writing a critique on the state of the world from an 'outside position' ('the God Trick', as she calls it) in order to identify the female (the Other), Haraway thus proposes that we write affirmatively, unconditionally and responsibly, drawing cartographies that do not start from a humanism but from urgent questions such as: 'What is to be done? What is it to live and die in a time of exterminations and extinctions and genocides?' (in Dolphijn 2012, 112).

It is the mapping of these ways of knowing *while* they realize and actualize themselves in troubling times, combined with a speculation upon their apparent futures, that Haraway now considers the new aim for feminist theorizations, or for new materialist and posthumanist theorizations, as we could also refer to them. It defines the notion of a feminist agency *not* enclosed in or captured by a *type* of subjectivity that needs to be defined female 'in-itself'. Rather, situated knowledges call for the geometer to explore the earth in a feminine way, both as an experiment and from experience, in the broadest sense, revealing the *activism-in-progress* that surrounds us. Its object of research is thus in every way both active and in change: 'Situated knowledges require that the object of knowledge be pictured as an actor *and* agent, not as a screen, or a ground, or a resource' (Haraway 1988, 592).

Haraway writes the feminist life deconstructed as an activist yet affirmative politics: a geometer activism *occupied with* feminism. Continuing/rewriting Derrida's critique of 'carno-phallogocentrism' as he referred to the human dominance over (animal) life on earth (see for instance Derrida 1992 and [2006] 2008), Haraway's situated knowledges take us to the ethical and political questions of the contemporary: 'if social, emotional, and cognitive complexity is the criterion. Derrida got it right. There is no rational or natural dividing line that will settle on the life-and-death relations between human and nonhuman animals; such lines are alibis if they are imagined to settle the matter "technically"' (Haraway 2008b, 297). The feminism she has to offer us, heavily inspired by currents in contemporary biology and the life sciences, does not stick to critiquing these alibis but shows the transversal lines that run through life *and* death, human *and* animal, nature *and* culture, man *and* woman.

Haraway (2007b, 2) shows that deconstructive critique, as she calls it, of modernist (Cartesian or Kantian) dualisms maps the cracked earth, the wounds that mark us *and* our surroundings:

> There is no border where evolution ends and history begins, where genes stop and environment takes up, where culture rules and nature submits, or vice versa. Instead, there are turtles upon turtles of naturecultures all the way down. Every being that matters is in a congeries of its formative histories – all of them – even as any genome worth the salt to precipitate it is a convention of all the infectious events cobbled together into the provisional, permanently emerging things Westerners call individuals, but Melanesians, perhaps more presciently, call dividuals.

It is upon this non-dualist trail that Barad pursues her deconstructive critique, continuing the way in which Haraway and Derrida deconstruct carno-phallogocentrism. Taking seriously the idea 'that subjectivity is not the exclusive prerogative of anthropos' (Braidotti 2013, 82) nor of any 'organic culture', Barad opens it up to the Great Outside, introducing critical theory to nature as a whole: to physics.

Accepting the Harawayan neologism naturecultures as a most fitting alternative to this dualism, Barad pushes materialist thinking even further away from the Anthropos, introducing us to a feminism that is not focusing on rethinking biology or the life sciences in particular but on the natural sciences as a whole. To summarize Haraway's position:

> What is *to be* is at stake. How to become-with is at stake. And it matters; it matters who does what. Cynicism is *not* an acceptable position in the face of the crisis that we are in, but 'staying with the trouble' is. And it involves aesthetic, cognitive, literary, technical, sensual – all with depths of thinking, sensing, feeling, bearing, acting.
>
> (Haraway in Dolphijn 2012, 110)

Haraway is fundamentally interested in being and becoming, which Barad fully affirms. Yet, although agreeing with Haraway, my argument would be that the non-dualist deconstructivism of Barad starts changing the Heideggerian interest in 'being-in-the-world', as it drove Derrida and to a lesser degree Haraway, into a 'being-of-the-world'. In other words, by not (implicitly) starting from an idea of subjectivity (and its attendant idea of objectivity) and by not (implicitly) situating life *in* the world (surrounded by the world, by Others), Barad makes critical theory an earthly, or perhaps even natural, enterprise. Deconstructive critical theory, with Barad, thus does not wait for the human to begin: it has always already been *of* the earth.

With Haraway we were searching for other forms of feminist subjectivity *in situ* (from *sinere* (lat.), 'putting down'). We may refer to this as a *relative* form of feminism, as it searches for 'a different view'. Searching for a way to get beyond an idea of subjectivity and its complex, anthropocentric history, Barad introduces us therefore to 'agential realism', as she refers to it. Agential realism reverses Haraway's situated knowledge. It emphasizes ontology instead of epistemology (stressing 'the real' instead of 'knowledge') and by that offers us a materialist feminism that is *absolute*. It is not so much in search for different views (alternative perspectives, critiquing Other forms of knowledge) but rather focuses on sameness (every reality is and can only be agential). Less activist than Haraway's call to situate knowledge (which is also aimed at those theorists who refused to do so), Barad's agential realism, technical and analytical, proposes that we study the real *only* through what we may call 'its contractions'.

Barad explicitly says that it is in this sense that her work practices a different feminism than Haraway's. When we asked her how she saw her 'manifesto' end up in contemporary cultural theory, she replied:

Well, manifesto is a thing that my friend and colleague Donna Haraway can get into, but I cannot claim that term. [Laughs.] Of course, she means it ironically. Agential realism is not a manifesto, it does not take for granted that all is or will or can be made manifest. On the contrary, it is a call, a plea, a provocation, a cry, a passionate yearning for an appreciation of, attention to the tissue of ethicality that runs through the world. Ethics and justice are at the core of my concerns or rather, it runs through 'my' very being, all being. Again, for me, ethics is not a concern we add to the questions of matter, but rather is the very nature of what it means to matter.

(Barad in Dolphijn and van der Tuin 2012, 70)

In light of such a claim, it is urgent to ask ourselves how this different feminist politics, which is not a difference feminism, then comes with a wholly other becoming. For although one could argue whether the book is presented as such, Barad's *Meeting the Universe Halfway* in the end maps a naturalism that is about engagement, about situatedness and about responsibility, appealing in particular to the sciences to reconnect ethically to 'the living present', as Derrida asks us to do. I agree here with the work of Joseph Rouse, who has noted Barad's 'feminist naturalism' and to whose work Barad often refers. In a footnote commenting on his work, Barad explains the link between normativity and naturalism:

> [M]y account of scientific practices is not naturalistic in the sense of giving science unquestioned authority to speak for the world, on the contrary; Rouse argues that a suitably revised conception of naturalism takes seriously what our best scientific theories tell us while simultaneously holding science accountable for its practices, for its own sake as it were, in order to safeguard its stated naturalist commitments.

> (Barad 2007a, 407n19)

Practicing a geophilosophy with a feminist ontology, Barad's quantum mechanical take on responsibility does not presuppose the human subject or the natural female body as the starting point for her *feminist* analysis (see also Rouse 2004, 155). Her 'agential realism' explores situatedness as a processual becoming in which things do not exist but come into existence with the material relations in which they are spun.

Contrary to the metaphysical naturalism in which concepts such as objectivity quickly lead to the acceptance of the Laws of Nature (think also of genetic coding or 'gene fetishists', as Haraway calls them (Haraway 1998, 189)), Barad's naturalism agrees with Haraway's 'naturecultures', which refuses to accept any nature outside of culture.

Donna Haraway and Karen Barad are, in this sense, very much in line with their European contemporaries Michel Serres and Isabelle Stengers, who are also rewriting physics from a materialist and non-human perspective. Serres is perhaps most critical of what 'laws' claim to say in post-Cartesian physics. He claims ([1990] 1995, 75):

> Law never gives orders and rarely writes or speaks in the imperative; nor does it designate, that is, write or speak in the indicative. It uses the performative. This means that truth, the conformity of the spoken or the prescribed with the facts, ensues immediately from its prescription or its speaking.

Practicing physics as an entanglement (see also Barad's concepts 'Getting Real' (1998) and 'material-discursive'), Barad's agential realism deconstructs these epistemic practices (necessarily dualist) as they organize our thinking from quantum physics (e.g. Schrödinger's cat, see Barad 2007a, 284) to feminist theory (e.g. Butler's theory of performativity, idem, 208). Barad notes that naturalism, in general, has the tendency to keep the opposition between nature and culture intact (idem, 463n104).

Mapping material intra-actions that traverse the organic and the inorganic and the ideas to which they give rise, she often employs the term 'posthumanism' rather than naming this a critical naturalism. She does, however, admit that these terms signal something similar when she claims, 'Posthumanism, in my account, can be understood as a thoroughgoing critical naturalism, an approach that understands humans as part of nature and practices of knowing as natural processes of engagement with and as part of the world' (idem, 331–2).

Preferring to develop her ideas in posthumanist terms, instead of via a critical naturalism, surely follows the feminist potential of the former concept, which Braidotti (2013, 2019) analyses in greater detail. Thus, Barad teams up with an increasingly large group of scholars that consider it of the greatest importance to show that dualist thinking is the greatest error of contemporary thought. Barad's response is a quantum mechanics that is at the same time *necessarily* a posthuman feminism. Starting from intra-action, the creative powers from which any type of epistemological individuality is being composed, she signals the birth of a particle, of a wave, an apparatus and a (female) body in whatever form, taking place *only* as contractions in a surface.

Following Braidotti, surpassing the Kantian Subject (with a capital S), geophilosophy needs a new theory of subjectivity, in line with feminist politics and the future of feminist theory. In Braidotti's work, too, a new theory of the Subject cannot be considered separately from a critical naturalism. She rightfully insists on a posthumanism that does not so much follow Foucault's earliest writings (*Les Mots et Le Choses*, his *Introduction* to Kant's *Anthropology*, in which he famously critiques Kant's Subject and the anthropocentrism this entailed) but, rather builds upon the unfinished biopolitical analyses that we find in the *History of Sexuality* and in his lectures at the College de France which have only recently been published. Rereading Foucault's emphasis on the 'care of the self' (as developed in this later work), Braidotti (2013, 116) summarizes the pros and the cons of a Foucauldian Posthumanism in our age:

> The advantage of such a position is that it calls for a higher degree of lucidity about posthuman bio-organic existence, which means that the naturalist paradigm is definitely abandoned. The disadvantage of this position, however, is that it perverts the notion of responsibility towards individualism.

The bio-ethical citizenship Braidotti seeks, which marks the posthumanism we also find in Barad, opts for a type of subjectivity that aims at a sustainable, ecological or relational construction of subjectivity. It is a type of subjectivity that does not demand that the human mind be the 'checkpoint' necessary to verify everything there is, upon which post-Kantian thought, or 'correlationism' as Meillassoux calls this, insisted. Barad's quantum physical-ethical subjectivity responds by *rewriting* this naturalist paradigm, offering us all forms of (female) subjectivities that are by all means 'of the world'. Barad's posthumanism thus searches for subjectivities that we encountered before, in, for instance, the work of Gregory Bateson, particularly in his 1972 masterpiece *Ecology of Mind*, where he nicely summarizes the urgency of thinking through intra-action (491–2):

> When you narrow down your epistemology and act on the premise 'What interests me is me, or my organization, or my species,' you chop off consideration of other loops of the loop structure. You decide that you want to get rid of the by-products of human life and that Lake Erie will be a good place to put them. You forget that the eco-mental system called Lake Erie is part of your wider eco-

mental system – and that if Lake Erie is driven insane, its insanity is incorporated in the larger system of your thought and experience.

The ethics practiced here by Bateson shows the re-(con)figurations that realize themselves in the events we live, demonstrate, in very simple terms, how posthumanism should be a kind of critical naturalism. Yet by emphasizing critical naturalism, Bateson has accurately foreseen what, in our time, has become a much needed theoretical (and therefore ethical) debate.

Living in the era sometimes referred to as the 'Anthropocene', a term with which Dutch Nobel Prize winner Paul Crutzen (2002) marks the times in which humanity is the geological force responsible for fundamental changes in the bio-sphere, the political necessity for a critical naturalism is perhaps the most pressing in contemporary cultural theory. Interestingly enough, Crutzen, himself a geologist/ chemist, has shown us that human dominance is not limited to the way technology has alienated itself from natural processes but also includes the fact that humanity, in many ways (including those both social and economic), increasingly opposed itself (Subject) to the world (Object) it intended to master.

Implicitly, Crutzen's claim confirms that dualism lies at the heart of the Anthropocene. Dualism is central to what Foucault would consider the condition for our truth: it marks our time and it has done so throughout modernity (see Foucault 1966, ch. 2). At the start of the twentieth century, mathematician and philosopher Whitehead ([1925] 1967) shows us how this dualism was at work long before the Industrial Revolution via the writings of fellow mathematician and philosopher Descartes. As mentioned before, Whitehead sees the devastating effects of modern factories on the (English) landscape and already warned us that what Crutzen would later call the Anthropocene follows from a state of mind rather than from individual ideas:

> The general conceptions introduced by science into modern thought cannot be separated from the philosophical situation as expressed by Descartes. I mean the assumption of bodies and minds as independent substances, each existing in its own right apart from any necessary reference to each other.
>
> (Whitehead [1925] 1967, 194)

Or to sum up the argument of this analysis, reflecting actually the opening paragraphs of this book: dualism, in every way, created the modern world as we know it.

The critical naturalist ethics that Barad develops is, therefore, timely. Performing the ecological through both science and the humanities (in quantum physics and in feminism), she shows such dualisms as the condition for truth in our times. Yet by dismantling them, stressing the intra-active, positing her critical naturalism along the way, she shows how epistemic networks place different cuts (agential cuts as she calls them), *creating* the subject, the object, the medium (2007, 352). Her quantum mechanics *is* a critical naturalism *is* a posthuman geophilosophy. It reveals us an earth of intra-actions, of agential cuts and of sorority. Or as she concludes herself:

> My posthumanist elaboration of Bohr's account understands the human not as a supplemental system around which the theory revolves but as a natural phenomenon that needs to be accounted

for within the terms of this relational ontology. This conception honours Bohr's deeply naturalist insight that quantum physics requires us to take account of the fact that we are part of that nature which we seek to understand.

(2007, 352)

The geometers first axiom: A body is that which folds

In *the Birth of Physics*, Serres notices what he calls a 'history of the angle'. It is his way of summarizing a physics which has not (yet) surrendered to the number, to quantification, to particular forms and bodies that represent the matters of life. The 'magicians of logic', as Erasmus calls those who defend the present status quo – the priests, the humanists, the capitalists – in his *In Praise of Folly*, perhaps recalling Dante's *Inferno* where the devil famously tells us: *tu non pensavi ch'io loico fossi* (you didn't know that I was a logician)? Magicians armed with The Number, who will always start (and end) with Ideal Forms (triangles, rectangles) designed to dominate and who confuse rigour with exactitude, as Serres puts it. The good news: another physics is possible. In fact, this wholly other non-Cartesian physics has not just seen the light with the rise of twentieth-century quantum physics and quantum mechanics but has been at work all along. Long before Niels Bohr there was the physics of Lucretius, of Archimedes, of the lever and of the screw and of many more geophilosophers that spent their life in anonymity all over the world, long before philosophers of science like Joseph Needham proved the short-sightedness of (Western) academia. It is the physics that was dear to so many people in the world, before (during and after!) European dominance. It is the physics that revealed the most impressive temples and hid the most extensive necropolises. It is the physics that explains the construction of the *Anji* Bridge, built around 600 in China's Hebei province, a bridge that spans over thirty-seven metres. A distance that engineers in Europe, masters of exactitude, could only cover for the past 120 years.

Spinoza says it all: we do not know yet what the body can do. In a breath-taking part of the Ethics, which starts in part two after proposition thirteen, Spinoza gives the geometer their toolbox. Among Spinozists it is referred to as his 'small physics'. This is not a philosophy of the body. It is a philosophy of what the body can do. In other words, as Serres would call it: it is a philosophy of the angle. It deals with movement and slowness and motion and rest, on unifying and on separating, on magnitude and on the lightness of being. The geometer, equipped with their Spinozist tools, is the choreographer, who constructs, moves and bends, what matters with these tools.

In a personal conversation with Brian Massumi, choreographer William Forsythe said just that, when he stated that 'a body is that which folds' (Massumi 2011a, 140). Intrigued by returning issues like 'How can we tell the dancer from the dance?' (see Colebrook 2005), Forsythe's idea of the body offered Massumi a way to differentiate contemporary from modern dance. Warding off any emphasis on representation and on using the body as a means to express an inner feeling as this often occurs in modern dance – Massumi specifically mentions Martha Graham's symbolic use of gesture (see for instance Graham 1937) – contemporary dance, he claims, intends 'to focus on pure movement' (Gil 2002, 121, quoted in Massumi 2011a).

It is a crucial difference: whereas in modern dance the body dances (bodily movements create the dance), the dancer in contemporary dance comes to be *in* the dance (movements create a dancing body). An epic example of the latter would be Pina Bausch's *Café Müller*, where the chairs in the café did not surround the dancer, creating the mise-en-scène in front of which the dancer danced: the legs of the chairs are involved in the dance no less than the legs of the dancer. The dance happens in what matters, in the intra-action between all that matters (per)forms.

Forsythe's definition indeed shows us that contemporary dance overcomes the dualisms that gave form to modernity/modern dance. On the one hand, it has no interest anymore in the opposition between the dancer and the world (which it was supposed to re-present or dance-to). Contemporary dance does not consider the body 'already in existence', filled with potentialities to be realized whenever the situation (the dance) asks it to. On the contrary, the body happens in the dance, which means that it is *only* through the act of folding (the dance) that it (the body, the fold) realizes itself. Also, this means that the folding actualizing a bodily whole does not follow from an Aristotelian idea of memory or from any agency that is supposed to organize the body in advance. Rather, the body-mind happens *in* the folding, which is to say that it is only because of the folding that its unity appears. A body takes shape, as does its idea.

The moment of individuation has been central in the philosophy and psychology of Gilbert Simondon (1992b: 311, *own translation*), who stated:

> Instead of grasping individuation using the individuated being as a starting point, we have to grasp the individuated being from the viewpoint of individuation, and individuation from the viewpoint of preindividual being, each operating at many different orders of magnitude.

Directed against modernist philosophy (and physics, biology and psychology), Simondon's refusal of an anthropocentric genesis that works backwards (presuming a history) rather favours an ontogenesis of the contemporary, anticipating realization of futurity. Simondon makes a similar (contemporary) plea for pure movement, for immanence and for thinking in terms of folds.

The proposal to start our thinking outside of the modernist propositions is nicely conceptualized by Forsythe's use of 'the fold'. For it is the fold, first and foremost, which is telling us that the body, even at the moment it appears to us (the realized moment of resemblance), should *not* to be considered an inside that can be opposed to an (or its) outside. Remembering Serres' physics of the angle, Deleuze's fold tells us how to rethink the body as that which folds, when stating, 'The outside is not a fixed limit but moving matter animated by peristaltic movements, folds and foldings that altogether make up an inside: they are not something other than the outside, but precisely the inside of an outside' ([1986] 1988: 98). In his choreography *One Flat Thing, Reproduced*, Forsythe (2006) shows us best how dance can dissolve a fixed, geometric, grid of tables into a topological surface in movement according to a series of synchronous folds and foldings (clustered bodies, contrapuntal bodies, complexes, curving nets, differentiations, etc.).

Rejecting the difference between inside and outside altogether is probably the only way to stress how radically contemporary dance focuses on pure movement. Dance cannot be captured by bodily codes, its expressionism cannot be limited by signs and its movements cannot be reduced to Vitruvian schemas. Contemporary dance is not about 'meaning' nor does it 'resist' anything, as Allbright still claims (1997, xiv). Legendary performer Merce Cunningham, already in the early 1960s, made it all too clear when claiming:

> There's no thinking involved in my choreography. I work alone for a couple of hours every morning in the studio. I just try things out. And my eye catches something in the mirror, or the body catches something that looks interesting; and then I work on that.... I don't work through images or ideas – I work through the body.
>
> (in Tomkins 1965, 246)

More explicitly than Forsythe, Cunningham was very outspoken in his rejection of the modern tradition, especially its emphasis on schemes 'That sort of A-B-A business based on emotional or psychological meanings just seemed ridiculous to me' (in Tomkins 1965, 244).

Cunningham beautifully explains how contemporary dance does not start with the body but with the feeling of *all* matter, *every* form to be actualized and realized in the dance to come. Getting rid of modernism then also means getting rid of the body as the point of departure for dance to happen. As José Gil put it: 'energy circulates directly in space rather than from the body to things' ([Gil [1985] 1998, 145). Contemporary dance is to feel the unforeseen, to allow the unexpected vibrations to kick in. Its point of departure should therefore be what Gil later referred to as 'the intense exterior' (2006, 24).

In the intense exterior, all matter *has to be* opened up, one way or another, by a continuous myriad of forces that we could call 'the dance'. This is what Massumi refers to as the speculative nature of contemporary dance. Every movement, every posture, comes with a movement to come, and gives us a promise never to be redeemed. Dance can no longer be a move from one gesture to the next, since in-between, always already, something happens, a movement is broken up: unforeseen intensities keep on (un)folding all that matters into new bodies and that is actually key to what the dance is. Keeping this in mind, we cannot but conclude that there is no reason to analyse contemporary dance necessarily in its relation to the modern tradition. The intense exterior is about the possible breaking up of *all* movement, about transforming of all of the geometrical surfaces into topological planes, testing their unknown elasticities. There is no reason to relate this to modern dance, or to any other tradition in particular, as in the end, every possible tradition can be broken up and must be. The intense exterior refuses any predetermined relationality at all, and therefore, it is *necessarily* at work in all possible traditions. The intense exterior is the undercurrent in all traditions that is about to crack it open and to reveal it otherwise.

In order to feel how the folding starts, how matter is opened up and (per)formed in contemporary dance, let us look more closely at a scene in contemporary dance practice in which this intense exterior is at work. I propose to analyse a scene from the performance *Ghost Track* by LeineRoebana. It is an intra-action between the dancers, Tim Persent and Boby Ari Setiawan, and the contemporary gamelan music played by Iwan Gunawan and his *Kyai Fatahillah* orchestra. The compositions and improvisations of Gunawan in many ways recall Karl-Heinz Stockhausen's orchestral works (the gamelan orchestra is as diverse as any contemporary symphony orchestra with its woodwind, brass, percussion, strings and, today, electronics sections), though its emphasis on percussion (metallophones, xylophones and drums) already proves how the history of gamelan (much more so than the symphony orchestra) entangles with a history of dance (and with a history of martial arts and a history of theatre). Gunawan's rhythms are thus not the rhythms 'to be danced to'; they do not set the body into motion: they *are* the rhythms always already traversing matter, the movements of the hands and of the eyes. The syncopating and polyrhythmic chants *are* the dimensionalities and directionalities according to which the rituals are set out in space. The acceleration and deceleration of the pulse keep on altering qualitatively the proper intervals in which the bodies happen.

The contemporary pulses and the peristaltic movements that dance the matters involved traverse patterns from the modern traditions and from the traditions from Central Java. In the beginning, they still (slowly) skirt around each other. Both dancers are facing the audience, standing belly to back, as one dancer firmly attaches to the ground slowly shifting his balance from left to right, while another rises to the sky, searching for ways to fall into the emptinesses created while being pulled out of them at the same time. The former dances a *kreasi baru*, a 'new creation' which comes down to a recreation of, or an improvisation upon (*nandhak*), various narrations (*greget*) found in the old central Javanese and Sundanese tradition. The latter is bound to rewrite the heritage of ballet, the relatively recent fulcrum of so many Occidental dancing styles. But as the experiment progresses, both traditions get tangled up into one another. Both traditions turn out impossible to 'maintain'. Lines intertwine, the breaking up of movements is unavoidable, cracks are appearing and the one *has to* bleed into the other and vice versa. And this is where the intense exterior kicks in.

During several of the public discussions I had with Harijono Roebana, one of the choreographers (the other being Andrea Leine), he kept on insisting that he (and his Occidental dancers) knew very little about all the different and rich traditions in Indonesian dance. Similarly, the Indonesian dancers were not aware of how modern dance worked. Themes were not copied and narrations were not retold. The pulses and the peristaltic movements that became more and more forceful, more and more persistent throughout the dance, slowly but steadily broke open the traditions and all that they presumed. There was no pattern of interaction, no understanding, no anticipation possible. Something new had to step in, generated from the various individual movements as they clashed. A new system that *included* the dancers as well as the musicians and their instruments was actualized. And it had to be kept in movement not by the dancers or the musicians but by this larger entity, by the entire system, by the dance itself. The new information causing this learning process came 'only from *within the system*', as Bateson articulates it (2002, 130): 'There has been a change in boundaries.'

The abstract relations felt in the intense exterior modify a dance in any possible way. The two dancers extend each other's movements, folding and unfolding them, creating the unforeseen new bodies that make up the new dance, the contemporary dance. The old does not disappear but is fragmented and taken up into the new: the movements of the (over)stretching of the fingers (*ngithing*) aimed at creating figures like 'the full moon' and 'the crescent moon' are now broken off only to be continued by the upper arm of the other dancer or in the sonorous sound of the gong.

Still facing the audience, the two dancers, the two traditions, open up. Arms entangle; movements flow from one hip to another chest, from one left to the other right, searching for diagonals that resonate, placing pressure, pushing and pulling together. This happens through what Spuybroek could have called the 'stepwise procedure of iterative adjustments based on the minimalization of difference' (2011, 22); in other words, the smallest variation sets out to make entirely new figures – J-curves, S-curves, giving rise to new bodies that never happened before. The dance never follows the potentials of the body of the dancer; it does not 'respect' what the body can do. On the contrary: oppositions between the important and unimportant, the approximate and the distant are all broken up *and* smoothened. Every dance creates a new diagram, a new set of functives, of textures *inhabiting* the matters involved, drawing them out anew.

Ghost Track shows us that the intense exterior, as it signals contemporary performance, is at work everywhere. As could be expected, given its topological nature, the intense exterior has the potential of breaking up all matter, every aspect of that-which-is-about-to-happen. In the dance discussed above, this is precisely how the intense exterior is at work. A dancer or a tradition or any possible body becomes 'a target' not because it *knows* the Other, opens up or reaches out for 'it'; on the contrary, the radical openness is all about *seducing the entire totality of exterior forces* to kick in. The chemistry of radical openness is pure bodily experimentation for only then that radical change of boundaries can occur, only then folds or bodies can happen anywhere. Then, it breaks open the dancers, the modern traditions, the traditions from Central Java and all that matters, to play a role. The intense exterior breaks open any dance. Its unforeseen new folds, its unknown new figures can be actualized everywhere, every time. For the intense exterior, though crucial to contemporary dance is by no means limited to events that happen in our time. The intense exterior is a very powerful transversal force that easily folds its way across times and spaces breaking up all of those bodies willing to become a target, willing to be broken up.

There is good reason why *Ghost Track* perseveres in breaking up the modern traditions *and* the Central Javanese ones. For as the intense exterior is invented time and again, this, not in the least place, cracks open the Central Javanese performance traditions. We already mentioned that in these traditions there could never have been an *l'Art pour l'Art* movement, as not so much the melody and harmony but rather the tempo and (most of all) the density (*Irama*) of the performance happens in the music, in the dance and in the storyline. But in Central Java, this tempo and this density also involve religion, martial arts and sociopolitics. The acceleration and deceleration of the performance most of all find their fulcrum in the particular folded nature of the orchestra.

Unlike the doubled Baroque orchestras (two halves that were most of the time identical to one another), the two parts of the Central Javanese Gamelan orchestra have no knowledge of one another whatsoever. They are indeed two radically different orchestras that fold into one another, that turn into one body because they move together. Known as the *slendro* (a five-tone tuning) and *pelog* (a seven-tone tuning) system, each ensemble consists of two uniquely tuned groups of instruments that break each other up only through the density of the composition. Indeed, they do not open themselves up to the Other system; they are *being cracked up by* this intense outside.

Both Michel Serres ([1983] 2013) and Gilles Deleuze ([1988] 1993) see an analogy in how the baker stretches and folds its dough and how time is folded into memory, into thought. This is exactly how ideas, or 'meaning' if we want to hold on to that word, happen in the dance. As the folding connects one end of the dough to the other and merges them, movement should not be reduced to a linear development but concerns all sorts of contractions and attenuations that form the body. Folding matter, folding what matters, contemporary dance always thinks otherwise. When Gil, in his thinking of dance, then concludes that 'the meaning of movement is the very movement of meaning' (2002, 125), he shows us the power of creative thought.

The geometer maps that which is savage, irregular, alive

In his book *The Sympathy of Things*, Lars Spuybroek revitalizes the word 'sympathy' as a means to show how form and life need to be studied aesthetically, analysing 'what things feel when they shape each other' (2011, 9). Spuybroek, himself a highly praised architect (with his office Nox), who, in the 1990s and in the 2000s, designed and built acclaimed designs such as the *HtwoOexpo Waterpavilion* in the Netherlands, the *Maison Folie* in Lille and the *Oblique WTC* for New York (not realized) and interactive artworks such as *D-tower* in Doetichem and *Son-O-House* in Son en Breughel. His writings accompany his designs, as all of his work studies the intra-action between the built environment and the different ways to live it.

Interestingly enough, 'sympathy' was not (yet) 'humanized' at the end of the nineteenth century. Sympathy might happen between us and a vase, between a wasp and an orchid, between the oceans and the moon. Sympathy highlights all of these processes of sameness, showing us an earth that is warmer, friendlier and more fraternal and sororal. It's a most useful concept for the geometer trying to map the twenty-first-century earth overgrown by capitalism. Spuybroek shows us how, in architecture, the undecorated empty white cube has for long been a false ideal, a deadly idea even, to speak with Arakawa and Gins: a transcendentalism that had very little to do with how *life* takes place, or, that had very little to do with the earth. Finding his soulmates in Romantic aesthetics, their architecture, their ideas on design, as it was always involved with the sympathy of things (to come).

Romanticism, with its eye for wildness and wilderness, can be found in Fichte's idea that aesthetics is the necessary starting point for the understanding of any 'spirit', or, in Herder when he states: '[O]nly inner sympathy, i.e., feeling and transposition of our whole human self into the form that has been explored by touch, is the teacher and indicator of beauty' (in: Spuybroek 2011, 147). Finding our way back to beauty equals finding our way back to life, out of idealism and perhaps even out of modernism (the white cube) as a whole, as it dominated the twentieth century in architecture *and* society at large. Exploring the fundaments of beauty/life means opening ourselves up (again) to the pleas of matter, to the creative forces of the unforeseen and the ever-changing imagery that it possibly produces.

Studying sympathy, let's follow Spuybroek following John Ruskin, in the appreciation of the Gothic as opposed to its 'idealist opposite', Roman Classicism (much more favoured by modernism). The Gothic ornament, in particular, needs our fullest attention.

We, modernists, all remember that it was the ornament which was explicitly and violently excluded from our built environment by modernism. Spuybroek reminds us that in search for the purification of the object, in search for the white cube, Adolf Loos wrote *Ornament und Verbrechen* (Ornament and Crime) and declared the ornament the enemy of form. Or to rephrase that in modernist terms: the ornament is *that which disturbs the Cartesian Line*. Spuybroek (through William Morris) rereads the ornament, so elementary to the Gothic, claiming that (2011, 77):

> Ornament is profoundly related to matter, to the way it structures itself as it undergoes forces, be they natural or technological, which is a complicated way of saying that ornament and texture share the traces of being made, of the constant reconfigurations of matter.

Ornaments, then, are not 'added to' a structure but should be seen as traces of its history, revealing the intra-action between the workers and the earth. Ornaments show the frictions, the folds of matter; they show the power of gravity and anticipate the elements.

So first of all, the ornament is the arrow, the vector between the history and the future of that which matters. In the Gothic especially, the opposition between ornament and structure, so important to modernist ethics, makes no sense: 'in the Gothic, *ornament acts like structure and structure acts like ornament*' (idem, 44, emphasis in original)). Gothic ornamentation is about entanglement, through the ornament, tesselation (from two to one dimension) and ribboning (from one to two dimensions) *make* spatiality.

Secondly, it is the arrow that orients the form of the design. The Gothic is all about the transformations, as ornaments traverse what matters in the design: 'It is not only a changefulness of columns, vaults, or traceries in themselves, but also one in which *columns transform into vaults into traceries'* (idem, 25). In more mathematical terms, praising variability, we need to conclude: 'Variability *within* an element leads to variability *between* elements. This makes the Gothic more radical than any other architectural style up to the present day' (idem, 26).

Spuybroek calls this the *digital* nature of gothic. The digital here is not a term owned by electronic computing but refers to the type of variation that is key to the binary code, but is just as much key to the Gothic. It comes down to the fact that the simple behaviour of individual elements (the smallest geometrical modulations that practice a 'difference in degree') leads to irreducibly complex collective behaviour, a new and unique beauty that reveals a 'difference in kind' (echoing the work of Henri Bergson). The digital links to the mannerist in his use of the term; through the finger or the hand (the respective Latin roots of both terms), Spuybroek stresses that architecture is not about abstract forms and surfaces. Architecture is not all about 'elements' (like floors and walls and windows), as Rem Koolhaas seems to think in his last book (2018). On the contrary: architecture is about the earth, about rediscovering the earth, about experimenting with it, playing with it. It is about feeling the earth, its strengths, its weaknesses.

Architecture, as Dubuffet also claims, is the first *art brut*. Spuybroek, after Ruskin, calls this the *savageness* of the Gothic:

'Savage' describes the workmen, the rough northern laborers, with their hands freezing, their heads in the mist and their feet in the mud, inevitably making 'mistakes' in their carving because of their 'rude' nature but also because of the open design system of the Gothic, which at certain points leaves them to decide what to do, or to hesitate suddenly and ultimately present us with 'failed, clumsy' ornament.

(2011, 13/4)

Ruskin himself knew this all too well:

And in all things that live there are certain irregularities and deficiencies which are not only signs of life, but sources of beauty. No human face is exactly the same in its lines on each side, no leaf perfect in its loves, no branch in its symmetry. All admit irregularity as they imply change; and to banish imperfection is to destroy expression, to check exertion, to paralyze vitality. All things are literally better, lovelier, and more beloved for the imperfections.

(Ruskin 1854, 14)

In the 'patterns of interaction', as Gregory Bateson called them, all comes to be. To get rid of these patterns, to deny their existence, as Loos proposes, equals fascism, equals death. Gins and Arakawa's manifesto *Making Dying Illegal. Architecture against Death: Original to the 21st Century* stresses a similar vitalism claims that 'Choosing to live within a tactically posed surround/tutelary abode will be counted as an all-out effort to go on living' (2006, 25). This calls for infinite variation; this plea for the radically unforeseen is also Spuybroek's wish, when he concludes by stating, 'I long for the day when we can see objects forming, like pools of mud, flowers on a wall or clouds in the sky, as pure products in context of pure productivity' (2011,

333). Spuybroek, the Spinozist, who is not lured by the ideal objects but who explores the earthly grooves and deterritorializes them. With their hands, with the brush, with the computer, we realize the smallest variation and imagine the different kinds of life this would entail. Spuybroek, the geometer.

The geometer maps how art objects

Let us never mistake materialism for a quest for the object! In *Killing Commendatore*, a two-volume book of more than 1,000 pages, Haruki Murakami makes us think about the artwork and the object which it is believed to be/which it is believed to be about. The portraits that the protagonist paints, the quick sketches he makes of people he meets here and there, are all *too real* for the white surface, the canvas. For several years, Murakami's nameless main character makes portraits for a living. It is commissioned, not free work, so he does not want to refer to it as art.

That changes, however, when a rich neighbour – a flamboyant man named Menshiki – asks him to paint his portrait for a big sum of money, because he claims to have much respect for the (hidden) artistic talents of the protagonist and wants him to explore them in full. From that moment, many things happen at the same time, things that somehow seem to resonate with one another, but as always with Murakami all of these events refuse to point towards a distinct cause or effect. They all matter and they somehow keep on mattering (in a different way).

Because of the freedom that Menshiki gives him, because of the generous sum of money, because of everything that happens in-between, the portrait that the protagonist makes of Menshiki is nothing like the portraits he had painted before. The protagonist is confused and wonders whether his first (semi-free) artwork will be accepted by his Maecenas. But when he sees it for the first time, Menshiki says he finds it beautiful: 'truly amazing. How shall I put it: this is exactly the painting that I had in mind' ([2017] 2017, 303, *my translation*).

It is obvious that Menshiki does not mean that the painting is a proper physical reflection of his face, as if he is looking in a mirror. The text tells us that there is actually hardly any resemblance between the painting and the painted, except perhaps for the way the 'white' in the painting makes reference to Menshiki's white hair. The white, the absence, the non-colour, the nothingness is there in the painting, and somehow, it makes Menshiki's face emerge from the painting. This means to say that, through the eyes of the protagonist, 'it even seems as if Menshiki himself is *in* the painting' ([2017] 2017, 394 *my translation*). In the painting, in the abstract play of lines and colours, Menshiki resides. *Not outside of it.*

Perhaps, what Murakami is showing us is what Michel Serres calls reversed Platonism, when he asks us: 'Could reality be born from representation?' ([1987] 2015, 126). This might well be the case in Murakami's novel, as the painting, or better, the painted – whatever it is – *causes many things to happen.*

It has often been said that the artist doesn't choose the subject, but the subject chooses the artist. But that is still quite a meagre and obsolete way of rethinking how art really works. And much worse: it is, of course, still a deeply humanist claim. Deleuze and Guattari already told us that 'art does not wait for the human being to begin' ([1980] 1987, 320). Irrespective of the human being, of our dominant idea of time (our history, present and future), art is always already there and will always be. Its travels are in no way controlled by us. So why not conclude that reality is a product of representation, instead of the other way around? Or better maybe: why not conclude that reality is a product of some sort of (human or non-human) imagination?

This would mean that the portrait, that which is extracted from the landscape, sheds a light on someone or something (an Idea, a Metaphor, as Murakami would have it) in such a way that whatever is revealed *is not there yet*. And perhaps it is never there to come. *It holds a promise.* At the same time, however, this something *was there all along*. It mattered before; it was just left unnoticed. Meshiki's face was there, yet it was through the artwork that it came into existence, that it was expressed and realized materially. For that reason, the protagonist in Murakami's novel, calls painting a 'prehension of movement... a premonition that allowed itself to be depicted by me' ([2017] 2018, 214).

But how is the depiction taking place? How is 'the author', to bring in this classical theme of aesthetics, involved in realizing this prehension? Crucial, again, seems to be a kind of absence. Throughout Murakami's book, the protagonist tells us that he has lost something which he has been in search of ever since (see for instance Murakami [2017] 2018, 175). This *wound* that he refers to, in some ways, concerns the early death of his sister, an event that – in its emptiness – accompanies him in every step he takes. Perhaps it is the same wound that comes back time and again in the form of a rabbit hole (an obvious reference to *Alice*) and in the many other cavities that play such an important role in his work. This is a recurring theme in Murakami's oeuvre (see also [2010] 2012): *there is always the wholly other world that can be found on 'the other side'*. In the here and now, this wound, as I call it, reveals itself in the main character's inability to build up meaningful relationships with women, and perhaps it even brought about his love for portraits (as art, in a way, is also the art of remembrance – of the face in this case).

This wound, as we have discussed before, does not 'belong to' the artist. It could have been that we, too, lost our sister at a young age or perhaps we know people dear to us who experienced something like this. But more likely, we, too, feel how this crack surfaces into our inability to build meaningful relationships, how this causes us to remember the face, how an event like this traumatizes and, as an undercurrent, cracks through the weakest of surfaces. One does not have to be an artist to understand how faces express this best, how they reveal themselves cracked up from their histories, fragile in how they face the future. One does not even have to be human, for that matter, to share this experience.

But it is the artist who *has to* stick with this wound; it is the artist who has to explore all of its virtual and unforeseen potentialities.

Earlier in Murakami's book, the ex-wife of the protagonist tells him she carries a sketch with her that he made for her on their first date. She says: 'Once in a while, I take the drawing out to look at it again. It is beautifully drawn. It gives me the feeling that I am looking at my true self' (Murakami [2017] 2017, 56). And this is actually also what Menshiki concludes. He is fascinated by the portrait (that refuses to resemble), because it tells more of him than he could have imagined. Because at the limits of the artwork and this has nothing to do with the canvas, there *is more history and more future* than he can bear.

To consider an artwork an object or a thing is a mistake – an historical mistake. However, the fact that the artwork *is* not an object or a thing does not mean that an artwork cannot be *turned* into one. It is bad destiny whenever an artwork is forced to spend the rest of its days like that, displayed like a corpse in a mausoleum. Then, an artwork is placed under a bell jar, exhibited in Paris or Bangkok, stewing in its own sour air (to paraphrase Sylvia Plath). It happens all too often unfortunately, to amazing art. We see it suffocating in front of our eyes. It is an absolute tragedy.

The horror of objectification is by all means pursued by the History of Art, by definition a tragic enterprise. But also, all the archives, all the museums, are blinded by the same historical error: that art is about objects. And every time, obviously, this is done for political reasons. To objectify is to solidify society, to groove society, to territorialize 'a people' through its archive/'its objects'. Objects are always invented, are always produced by imagined communities, but they play a crucial role in the realization of the religious, humanist and capitalist equilibrium that makes up the present.

It is no coincidence that the modern museum (by all means a product of Western thought) is built up from spaces that have much in common with the square that faces the church, the *grand boulevards* that are made to face the enemy. Designed for capture, these means of power have been objectifying the city especially since the nineteenth-century city and more than ever today. Contemporary architecture, so dependent upon the nineteenth- and twentieth-century public eye, is all too often ripped from any form of creativity, from its savageness, its earthliness, not because of its iconic form but especially because of the behaviour it expects from Others.

Michel Serres claims that there are three kinds of (quasi-)objects that have been very good in stopping time, maintaining the status quo, in preventing change from happening. He refers to objects of religion, objects of war and objects of capitalism: from totems to arms to money. Interestingly enough, these objects, or quasi-objects as he sometimes calls them, do not act but rather require permanent action. The totem should not move but should stand still so it can be worshipped. Arms should not be used but should be stocked to prevent war. Money should not be spent, but should be owned.

Thus, power functions according to three types of objects are key to the religious, humanist and capitalist realities of the present, which I have placed at the centre of my analysis throughout this book. The present is always organized around these three objects (and their derivatives), and they draw the histories and the futures of all of power today. A history and a future that is by definition modern (and dualist and anthropocentric), of course, that could only have been invented by the 'new times' of modernity. Before modernity, both history and future did not exist.

That perverse relation which art has to the present! Religion would never have been as fundamental to social life if it was not for art. The priest hated the artist, as the artist hated the priest – despised their being. Of course, the priest would stay in power. But at the same time, he knew that the artwork would persist in traversing the dogmas of religion, whatever the priest would do. Look at the ecstatic and fantastic paintings from before, where God makes everything possible – from the wild and savage clay of Gothic architecture to lyrical clouds with angels and orgies.

The same goes for the warlord/the statesman. He knows he would never have made it without those territorializing rhythms that only the finest composers could come up with; without statues on squares, without palaces, without the right historiographers, they would be helpless. More so than weapons that were not supposed to be used, it was the wood and the iron of the drum, the copper of the brass, that gave content to the march/the warfare (in times of war *and* in times of peace). But there was also always the pen and genius interventions such as Picasso's *Guernica* and Hendrix's *Smashing of the Amps* (a.k.a. *the Star-Spangled Banner*), two artworks that will never stop in resisting any form of warfare.

This is no different for the capitalist entrepreneur. If we have any hope that the capitalist bell jar that suffocates the entire globe today is going to crack soon, we need art, art of the highest kind. Of course, in the contemporary arts (think of the bioarts, contemporary installation or performance art), there is always already a critique on contemporary capitalism and its ravishing ecological effects, but artworks from 'before' are just as well able to confront the present with the roar from the earth. From the Romantics to the Mannerists, there are innumerable artworks from the past that easily deterritorialize the fables of the present, of every possible present.

The tripartite distinction of objects that Serres offer us has, of course, been complicated into many different appearances of religion, war and capital. Perhaps they have gone so abstract these days that we should rephrase this distinction with the help of Piercian linguistics, concluding that there are iconic, symbolic and indexical forms of power. And they are grooving the present more than ever before. Art refuses to work with this present, since it does not function with the objects that make the present possible. Art is interested in *the exact opposite*. Instead of being halted by matter, its aim is really to set matter into perpetual movement. Art is the undercurrent, that unprecedented, this burst of creativity that materializes in spite of the present.

Art matters perpetually: art is not an object… *art objects.*

Earth – You are everywhere

Pain is truth, all else is subject to doubt!

In the opening of Coetzee's *Waiting for the Barbarians* (1982), Colonel Joll is a torturer and knows very well how the truth of the wound causes imagination, that is, all sorts of realities, to come into existence. Mo Yan, in novels like *Sandelwood Death* ([2001] 2013), writes about this unapologetically. Reaching the thousandth wound is the goal for the torturer *and* for the tortured. It is the ultimate work of art, for both to reach that point (without the tortured dying, without the torturer unable to finish the wounding). And let us be very precise in this: the art of the cutting hand (*guizi shou*) is *not* reducible to a relationship between a torturer and the tortured. There is nothing human about this practice anymore. On the contrary, it's a meticulous technology aimed at revealing the rivers of blood and the dragon's skin; it is the finest play ever staged, according to the epitaph: a tragedy obviously, with many different players on stage (with a double role for Time and Timing).

More interesting even: when Friday killed the great goat Andoar, turning him into a goat-kite, was he not releasing the kite from the goat? It was of the greatest importance to Friday that Andoar could fly. The goat had to fly! Similarly, one could say that the river was obstructed and needed to flow. The dragon's integumentary system wanted scales and not plain skin. A new surface had to be installed; its undercurrents had to flood the existing land in order for a new earth to appear. And life will resume, differently. 'Every Living being is a survivor' (Serres [1982] 1995; 135). Or, rewriting Descartes: 'I am in pain, therefore I change' (idem).

Pain is truth, the opening up, the cracking, is truth as it is not so much laying the 'origin' for thinking, but rather offers us the new land upon which new alliances, new resonances, new overtones and their ideas, can occur. Pain is what matters. Before the (quasi-)objects are re-installed by the priests, the statesmen, the capitalist, the new land is being explored, territorialized and deterritorialized – in its relation to the earth.

This relationship between territory and the earth is crucial for understanding how ideas rise from matter, how ideas only rarely concern the human being and how it is indeed the movement of ideas that makes thought interesting, alive. Thinking is necessarily thinking-in-the-margins. At the borders of Christianity, at the borders of the state and of capitalism, at the borders of Cartesianism perhaps, the geometers roam the land and the sea. There, where paganism, where indigenous knowledges roam the vast meadows, where grooves are nothing but scratches on the surface, pointing in another direction whenever the wind changes.

Revolutions do not happen at the heart of the empire (where everything is ordered to stand still), but at its margins (where all is movement). The long history of mumming is, in this case, telling.

'Mumming', coming from the Greek *mummo* (denoting a child's bugbear, or a frightening mask), was a folk practice absorbed in Italian masquerading and thereafter in other courtly entertainment known as masque since the sixteenth century, but has a much longer history (stretching out until today) outside of Christian High Culture. Originally, however, mummers were bands of masked persons who during winter roamed the territory, defying its grooves, its organization. Terrifying the children, demanding food from all the households in their way, wearing masks from the sea, with seaweed and fish skin, the mummers from, for instance, the north of Scotland (the Orkney Islands, the Shetland Islands), Faeroër and Iceland teamed up with mythical creatures of the sea around the start of the new moon and cracked the territory. Between human and animal, between day and night, between nature and culture, they searched for a new land, a new spring to arrive.

Throughout Murakami's oeuvre, figures emerge that are very well aware of the fact that they are only very sketchy consequences of things that took place here and now, in the past or in the future. They know that they are here because they 'happen' and that they will only be here while this is happening. Johnny Walker, in *Kafka on the Shore*, laughs about his own existence, as it is so dependent upon the cats, the night and the turning stone being in the wrong position. In *Killing Commandatore,* the protagonist keeps on referring to himself as 'merely an idea'. The matter through which this idea was realized was a figure on a painting, but only in the eyes of the main character. Commendatore is an idea that exists only for him. Or as Murakami puts it: an idea only comes into existence when another recognizes it and it takes its form accordingly (Murakami [2017] 2018, part 2).

In a similar way, Johnny Walker seems to have been realized only for Nakata. His love for cats, his love for the night as well as his search for the turning stone gives rise to evil Johnny Walker.

Both Johnny Walker and Commendatore remind me of the gate in Franz Kafka's famous parable *Before the Law*. There, the gate is both the cause and the effect of the story. A life unfolds from the gate to the (same) gate, staging its own necessity, its own actors, its own fatal history. The two figures staged by Murakami can therefore best be seen as 'moments'. We fear their arrival; we are relieved when they depart. They capture the narrative, situate the main character in it anew, endangering their existence. They are pure power, making subjects and objects, threatening life, welcoming death.

All through *Kafka on the Shore*, Nakata, the geometer, the undercurrent protagonist of this book, remembers why he keeps on travelling the earth: to turn the Entrance Stone. The stone divides, creates this side and the other side and captures us all in its organization. I remember a trip to Naples, where I touched the work of the sculptor Corradini. Veiling the sacred in stone, the stoned veil, was done with such care, with such precision. The folds re-veiled the sacred, offering a truth to me and to me alone. It was eternity which he graciously liberated from the rock that once surrounded it. Now, it was surrounded with words, with ideas, that extend it from an origin to a destiny. A time past and a time to come.

The stone of Nakata. Was it savage? Primitive? Unpolished? Preiconic, it seemed to serve a similar purpose to the stones of Corradini. Securing a territory. And a time.

The turning of the stone, whether in the novel or in the sculpture, is a deterritorialization. It changes not only matter but also the light as it hit it. The chiaroscuro. It pulls it out of its perspective. To what? An iconoclasm, it demolishes the territory; it destroys time. No more past, no more future. Leaving us in vain, we are left within a major crisis. What language do we speak? How can we live this wholly other earth that is now revealing itself to us?. Horology. The study of time.

At the margins of the present, where the flood retreats, the water and the land mix and become fertile and a new time announces itself, the pagan, animist and vitalist traditions that had always been at work, as the undercurrents of religion, humanism and capitalism, announce themselves. They howl, they squeak and they create the noise of the earth. They stand in the sun and drip purifying oil. They insist that we all become geometers. We have to travel to beyond where the Nile springs, search again for the land of the Hyperboreans. Under siege because of viruses, nationalism, capitalism and all the other crises of the contemporary, I wish for the earth that a new letter from Prester John will arrive soon.

And for everybody to understand, that whenever one lives the earth, one thinks it.

REFERENCES

Allbright, Ann Cooper. 1997. *Choreographing Difference: The Body and Identity in Contemporary Dance*. Middletown: Wesleyan University Press.

Artaud, Antonin. 1976. *Selected Writings*. Ed. Susan Sontag. Oakland: University of California Press.

Bachelard, Gaston. [1958] 1969. *The Poetics of Space*. Boston: Beacon Press.

Barad, Karen. 1998. Getting Real: Technoscientific Practices and the Materialization of Reality. *Differences: A Journal of Feminist Cultural Studies* 10.2: 87–126.

Barad, Karen. 2007. *Meeting the Universe Halfway: Quantum Physics and the Entanglement of Matter and Meaning*. Durham and London: Duke University Press.

Bateson, Gregory. 2000. *Steps to an Ecology of Mind*. Chicago: University of Chicago Press.

Bateson, Gregory. 2002. *Mind and Nature: A Necessary Unity*. Cresskill: Hampton Press Inc.

Bausch, Pina. May 1985. *Café Müller* [Choreography].

Blanchot, Maurice. [1959] 2003. *The Book to Come*. Stanford: Stanford University Press.

Braidotti, Rosi. 2007. '*Bio-power and Necro-politics: New Ways of Dying*': *Institute for Human Sciences*, University of Vienna, March 20.

Braidotti, Rosi. 2008. In Spite of the Times: The Postsecular Turn in Feminism. *Theory, Culture and Society* 25.6: 1–24.

Braidotti, Rosi. 2013. *The Posthuman*. Cambridge: Polity Press.

Braidotti, Rosi. 2019. *Posthuman Knowledges*. Cambridge: Polity Press.

Brecht, Bertolt and Kurt Weill. 1928. *Die Dreigroschenopfer* [Opera].

Borges, Jorges. [1989]1998. *Collected Fictions*. New York: Penguin Books.

Cache, Bernhard. 1995. *Earth Moves, the Furnishing of Territories*. Ed. M. Speaks. Cambridge and London: The MIT Press.

Carson, Rachel. [1962]2000. *Silent Spring*. London: Penguin Books.

Chamovitz, Daniel. 2012. *What a Plant Knows, a Field Guide to the Senses*. London New York: One World Publications.

Coetzee, J. M. 1982. *Waiting for the Barbarians*. New York: Penguin Books.

Colebrook, Claire. 2005. How Can We Tell the Dancer from the Dance? The Subject of Dance and the Subject of Philosophy. *Topoi* 24.1: 5–14.

Conway-Morris, Simon. 2003. *Life's Solution: Inevitable Humans in a Lonely Universe*. Cambridge: Cambridge University Press.

Crutzen, Paul. 2002. Geology of mankind. *Nature* 415. 23.

Deleuze, Gilles. [1969] 1990. *Logic of Sense*. London: Athlone Press.

Deleuze, Gilles. [1981] 2003. *Francis Bacon: the Logic of Sensation*. London and New York: Continuum.

Deleuze, Gilles. [1986] 1988. *Foucault*. London: Athlone Press.

Deleuze, Gilles. [1988] 1993. *The Fold*. Minneapolis: Minnesota University Press.

Deleuze, Gilles. [1990] 1995. *Negotiations*. New York: Columbia University Press.

Deleuze, Gilles. 2001. *Pure Immanence, Essays on a Life*. New York: Zone Books.

Deleuze, Gilles. [2002] 2004. *Desert Island and Other Texts 1953–1974*. Los Angeles, New York: Semiotext(e).

Deleuze Gilles and Félix Guattari. [1972] 1984. *Anti-Oedipus: Capitalism and Schizophrenia*. Minneapolis: University of Minnesota Press.

Deleuze Gilles and Félix Guattari. [1980] 1987. *A Thousand Plateaus: Capitalism and Schizophrenia*. Minneapolis: University of Minnesota Press.

Deleuze Gilles and Félix Guattari. [1991] 1994. *What Is Philosophy?* New York: Columbia University Press.

Derrida, Jacques. [1962] 1978. *Edmund Husserl's Origin of Geometry, an Introduction*. Lincoln, NE : University of Nebraska Press.

Derrida, Jacques. [1967] 1978. *Writing and Difference*. Chicago: Chicago University Press.

Derrida, Jacques. [1978] 1987. *The Truth in Painting*. Chicago: University of Chicago Press.

Derrida, Jacques. 1992. Force of Law, the Metaphysical Foundation of Authority. In: Drucilla Cornell, Michel Rosenfeld and David Carlson (eds), *Deconstruction and the Possibility of Justice*. London: Routledge, 3–67.

Derrida, Jacques. [2006] 2008. *The Animal That Therefore I Am*. New York: Fordham University Press.

Derrida, Jacques and Anne Dufourmantelles. [1997] 2000. *Of Hospitality*. Stanford: Stanford University Press.

Derrida, Jacques and Francois Ewald. 2001. 'A Certain Madness Must Watch Over Thinking' Refusing to Build a Philosophical System, Derrida Priviliges Experience and Writes Out of 'Compulsion'. A Dialogue around Traces and Deconstructions. In: Gert J. J. Biesta and Denise Egéa-Kuehne (ed) *Derrida and Education*. London: Routledge.

Deugd, Cornelis de. 1966. *The Significance of Spinoza's First Kind of Knowledge*. Assen: van Gorcum.

Dolphijn, Rick. 2012. Staying with the Trouble: Interview with Donna Haraway. In: *Yes, Naturally*. Rotterdam: NAi 010 Publishers, 108–15.

Dolphijn, Rick (ed.). 2018. *Michel Serres and the Crises of the Contemporary.* London: Bloomsbury.

Dolphijn, Rick and Iris van der Tuin. 2012. *New Materialism: Interviews and Cartographies.* Ann Arbor: Open Humanities Press/MPublishing.

Dolphijn, Rick and Rosi Braidotti (eds.). 2021 (forthcoming). *Deleuze and Guattari and Fascism.* Edinburgh: Edinburgh University Press.

Du Bois-Reymond Emil. 1883. Darwin and Copernicus. In: *The Popular Science Monthly*, June, 249.

Engels, Friedrich. [1891] 1976. *De oorsprong van het gezin, van het particuliere eigendom en van de staat.* Boom: Amsterdam.

Forsythe, William. 2006. *One Flat Thing, Reproduced.*

Foucault, Michel. 1966. *The Order of Things: An Archeology of the Human Sciences.* New York: Vintage Books.

Fraser, Murray. 2005. The Cultural Context of Critical Architecture. *The Journal of Architecture* 10.3: 317–22.

Freud, Sigmund. [1917] 2012. *A General Introduction to Psychoanalysis.* London: Wordsworth editions.

Gabriel, J. Philip. 2006. *Spirit Matters: The Transcendent in Modern Japanese Literature.* Honolulu: University of Hawaii Press.

Gao, Xingjian. [1990] 2001. *Soul Mountain.* New York: HarperCollins.

Gaukroger, Stephen. 1989. *Cartesian Logic: An Essay in Descartes' Conception of Inference.* Oxford: Oxford University Press.

Gil, José. [1985] 1998. *Metamorphoses of the Body.* Minneapolis: University of Minnesota Press.

Gil, José. 2002. The Dancers Body. In: Brian Massumi (ed), *Parables for the Virtual: Movement, Affect, Sensation.* Durham and London: Duke UP, 117–27.

Gil, José. 2006. Paradoxical Body. *TDR: The Drama Review* 50.4: 21–35.

Gins, Madeleine and Arakawa. 2006. *The Architectural Body.* Tuscaloosa and London: The University of Alabama Press.

Gins, Madeleine and Arakawa. 2006. *Making Dying Illegal.* New York: Roof Books.

Graham, Martha. 1937. Artist Statement. In: Jean Morrison Brown e.a. (ed), *The Vision of Modern Dance: in the Words of Its Creators.* Princeton: Princeton Book Company, 49–53.

Haraway, Donna. 1988a. Situated Knowledges: The Science Question in Feminism and the Privilege of Partial Perspective. *Feminist Studies* 14. 3. Autumn issue.

Haraway, Donna. 1998b. Picturing Science Producing Art. In: C. A. Jones and P. Galison (eds), *Deanimations: Maps and Portraits of Life Itself.* New York and London: Routledge.

Haraway, Donna. 2007. Introduction: A Kinship of Feminist Figures. In: *The Haraway Reader*. New York and London: Routledge, 1–7.

Haraway, Donna. 2008. *When Species Meet*. Minneapolis: The University of Minnesota Press.

Harman, Graham. 2011. *Quentin Meillassoux: Philosophy in the Making*. Edinburgh: Edinburg University Press.

Heidegger, Martin. 1977. *The Question Concerning Technology and Other Essays*. New York: Harper and Row.

Jung, C. G. 1960. Synchronicity: An Acausal Connecting Principle. In: *The Structure and Dynamics of the Psyche, Collected Works Vol 8*. London, New York: Routledge & Paul Kegan Ltd.

Karatani, Kōjin. [2012] 2017. *Isonomia and the Origins of Philosophy*. Durham and London: Duke University Press.

Kohn, Eduardo. 2013. *How Forests Think, Towards an Anthropology beyond the Human*. Oakland: University of California Press.

Koolhaas, Rem. 2018. *Elements of Architecture*. Berlin: Taschen.

Kundera, Milan. [1983] 2009. *The Unbearable Lightness of Being*. New York: Harper Perennial Modern Classics.

LeineRoebana. 2011. *Ghost Track* [Choreography].

Lucretius Carus, Titus. [1924] 1975. *De rerum natura* (On the Nature of Things). Cambridge (MA): Harvard University Press.

Luther, John. 2013. *Sila: The Breath Of The World* [Composition].

Malabou, Catherine. [2007] 2012. *The New Wounded*. New York: Fordham University Press.

Malabou, Catherine. [2009] 2012. *Ontology of the Accident: An Essay on Destructive Plasticity*. Cambridge: Polity Press.

Massumi, Brian. 2002. *Parables for the Virtual: Movement, Affect, Sensation*. Durham and London: Duke University Press.

Massumi, Brian. 2009. Technical Mentality Revised: Brian Massumi on Gilbert Simondon. *Parrhesia*, 7, 36–45.

Massumi, Brian. 2011. *Semblance and Event: Activist Philosophy and the Occurent Arts*. Cambridge: MIT Press.

Massumi, Brian. 2014. *What Animals Teach Us about Politics*. Durham and London: Duke University Press.

Meillassoux, Quentin. [2006] 2008. *After Finitude: An Essay on the Necessity of Contingency*. New York: Continuum.

Mishama, Yukio. [1956] 2000. *The Sound of Waves*. New York: HarperCollins

Michaux, Henri. [1972] 2002. *Miserable Miracle*. New York: NYRB.

Moreau, Pierre-Francois. 1994. *L'expérience et l'éternité*. Paris: Presses Universitaires de France.

Murakami, Haruki. [2002] 2005. *Kafka on the Shore*. New York: Knopf Publishing Group.

Murakami, Haruki. [2010] 2012. *1Q84* (Three Volumes). London: Vintage.

Murakami, Haruki. [2013] 2015. *Colorless Tsukuru Tazaki and His Years of Pilgrimage*. New York: Vintage Books /Penguin publishers.

Murakami, Haruki. [2013/14] 2018. *Men without Women*. London: Vintage UK.

Murakami, Haruki. [2017] 2017. *De moord op commendatore Deel 1: een idee verschijnt*. Amsterdam: Atlas Uitgeverij.

Murakami, Haruki. [2017] 2018. *De moord op commendatore Deel 2: metaforen verschuiven*. Amsterdam: Atlas Uitgeverij.

Negarestani, Reza. 2008. *Cyclonopedia: Complicity with Anonymous Materials*. Melbourne: Re.press.

Negarestani, Reza. 2011a. Contingency and Complicity. In: Robin Mackay (ed), *The Medium of Contingency*. London: Urbanomic in association with Ridinghouse.

Negarestani, Reza. 2011b. Drafting the Inhuman: Conjectures on Capitalism and Organic Necrocracy. In: Levi Bryant et al. (eds), *The Speculative Turn: Continental Materialism and Realism*. Melbourne: Re.press.

Negri, Antonio. 1970. *Descartes politico o della ragionevole ideologia*. Milano: Feltrinelli.

Nietzsche, Friedrich. [1908] 2009. *Ecce Home*. Mineola NY: Dover Publications.

Nishitani, Keiji. 1982. *Religion and Nothingness*. Berkeley CA: University of California Press.

Parr, Adrian. 2013. *The Wrath of Capital: Neoliberalism and Climate Change Politics*. New York: Columbia University Press.

Perec, Georges. 1999. *Species of Space and Other Pieces*. London: Penguin Books.

Petit, Susan. 1991. *Michel Tournier's Metaphysical Fictions*. Amsterdam: John Benjamins Publishing Company.

Pindar, Ian and Paul Sutton. 2000. Translators Introduction. In: Félix Guattari (ed), *The Three Ecologies*. New York: Continuum, 1–12.

Rouse, Joseph. 2002. *How Scientific Practices Matter: Reclaiming Philosophical Naturalism*. Chicago: University of Chicago Press.

Rouse, Joseph. 2004. Barad's Feminist Naturalism. *Hypatia* 19.1: 142–61.

Ruskin, John. 1854. *On the Nature of Gothic Architecture: And Herein of the True Functions of the Workman in Art*. London: Smith, Elder &Co.

Ruskin, John. 1869. *The Two Paths: Being Lectures on Art and Its Application to Decoration and Manifacture*. New York: John Wiley and Son Publishers.

Ruskin, John and John D. Rosenberg. 1963. *The Genius of John Ruskin: Selections from His Writings*. London and New York: Routledge.

Said, Edward. 1979. *Orientalism*. New York: Vintage Books.

Sartre, Jean Paul. [1947] 1948. *The Chips Are Down*. London: Lear.

Serres, Michel. [1977] 2000. *The Birth of Physics*. Manchester: Clinamen Press.

Serres, Michel. [1982] 1995. *Genesis*. Ann Arbor: University of Michigan Press.

Serres, Michel. [1983] 2013. *Rome: The First Book of Foundations*. London: Bloomsbury.

Serres, Michel. [1987] 2015. *Statues: The Second Book of Foundations*. London: Bloomsbury.

Serres, Michel. [1990] 1995. *The Natural Contract*. Ann Arbor: University of Michigan Press.

Serres, Michel. [1995] 2017. *Geometry: The Third Book of Foundations*. London: Bloomsbury.

Serres, Michel. [2009] 2014. *Times of Crisis: What the Financial Crisis Revealed and How to Reinvent Our Lives and Future*. London: Bloomsbury.

Serres, Michel. [2010] 2012. *Biogea*. Minneapolis: Univocal.

Serres, Michel. [2012] 2015. *Thumbelina*. New York and London: Rowman and Littlefield International.

Serres, Michel. 2015. *Le gaucher boiteux: Puissance de la pensée*. Paris: Le pommier.

Serrurier, Cornelia. 1930. *Descartes Leer en leven*. 's Gravenhage: Martinus Nijhoff.

Shaviro, Steven. 2009. *Without Criteria: Kant, Whitehead, Deleuze and Aesthetics*. Cambridge (MA) and London: The MIT Press.

Simondon, Gilbert. 1980. 'The Evolution of Technical Reality: Element. Individual and Ensemble'. *On the Mode of Existence of Technical Objects*. Canada: University of Western Ontario.

Simondon, Gilbert. 1992a. The Genesis of the Individual. In: Jonathan Crary and Sanford Kwinter (eds), *Incorporations*. New York: Zone Books, 297–319.

Simondon, Gilbert. 1992b. *L'individuation physique et collective*. Paris: Aubier.

Simondon, Gilbert. [2004] 2011. *Two Lessons on Animal and Man*. Minneapolis: Univocal.

Sorkin, D. 2008. *The Religious Enlightenment*. Princeton: Princeton University Press.

Spinoza, Benedict. [1677] 2001. *Ethics*. Ware, Hertfordshire: Wordsworth.

Spinoza, Benedict. 1995. *The Letters*. Indianapolis/ Cambridge: Hackett Publishing Company.

Spuybroek, Lars (ed.). 2004. *NOX, Machining Architecture*. London: Thames and Hudson.

Spuybroek, Lars (ed.). 2009. *The Architecture of Variation*. London: Thames and Hudson.

Spuybroek, Lars. 2011. *The Sympathy of Things: Ruskin and the Ecology of Design*. Rotterdam: Nai Publishers.

Tanizaki, Junichirō. [1933] 2001. *In Praise of Shadows*. London: Vintage Classics.

Tomkins, Calvin. 1965. *The Bride and the Bachelors: The Heretical Courtship in Modern Art*. New York: Viking Press.

Tournier, Michel. [1967] 1997. *Friday*. Baltimore: Johns Hopkins University Press.

Whitehead, Alfred North. [1925] 1967. *Science and the Modern World*. New York: Free Press.

Whitehead, Alfred North. [1929] 1978. *Process and Reality*. New York: Free Press.

Worringer, Wilhelm. 1964. *Form in Gothic*. Ed. Herbert Read. New York: Schocken Press.

Yan, Mo. [2001] 2013. *Sandelwood Death*. Norman: University of Oklahoma Press.

INDEX

1968 22, 54, 102, 108
1Q84 65–6, 79–82
9/11 48–9

Affect 11, 16, 96. *See Ethics, see Spinoza*
Agential realism 112–14, 118
Akigawa, Marie 8
Andoar 147–8
Anotherness 45–6, 48, 54–7, 65–6, 75. *See Otherness, see world without Others, see wholly other*
Anthropocene 117–18
Anthropocentrism 14, 17, 91, 97, 115
Anti-Oedipus 36, 102, 153
Aomame, Masami 8, 81–6, 88
Appetite 11, 25–8, 46
Arakawa and Gins 134, 137
Architecture 134, 136–7, 143, 145, 154–7
Arissa Asmarats, Antoni 76
Art 7–9, 17, 22, 28, 52, 76, 79. *See the arts of the cutting hand;* and *art brut* 136; and geophilosophy 88–9, 100–02, 105; and *l'Art pour l'Art* 130; and objects 139–46
Art of the cutting hand, the (*guizi shou*) 147
Artaud, Antonin 7, 52, 94, 101

Bachelard, Gaston 67–8, 76
Barad, Karen 17, 107, 108, 110–16, 118
Barthes, Roland 100

Bateson, Gregory 13, 35, 116–17, 128, 137
Bausch, Pina 123
Between the wood and the iron 28, 145
Blanchot, Maurice 94–5
Blood/bleeding 74–5, 128, 147
Borges, Jorge Luis 23
Bousquet, Joë 63, 97, 100
Braidotti, Rosi 7, 17, 22, 41, 102, 110, 115–16
Bruno, Giordano 99

Café Müller 123
Capitalism 31, 35–7, 43–50, 82, 87, 89, 134, 144–5, 148, 151
Carson, Rachel 19
Cats 69, 73–5, 83, 86, 149–50
Chiaroscuro 73, 151
Christ 27, 44
Christianity 44, 46–7, 148
Coetzee, J.M. 147
Contemporary, the 3, 9, 21, 85–9, 124, 127; and crises 101, 105, 110, 151; and feminism 108, 110, 112; and the present 96
Contemporary dance 122–3, 125–6, 129–31
Copernicus, Nicolaus 97–8
Corona/the virus 19, 89, 151
Corradini, Antonio 150
Correlationism 116
Crack, the 56, 63, 81–6, 88–9, 92, 94, 95–7, 99–102, 105; and

contemporary dance 126, 128,
130–1; and Murakami 8, 65, 75,
80; and the present 9; and the
wound 142, 145, 148–9
Creative act, the 3, 52, 86–8
Critical naturalism 114–15, 117–18
Critical theory 110, 114
Critique 3, 69, 101, 105, 107–10, 115,
145; and Cartesianism 11, 28, 99;
and critique upon the critique 28
Crutzen, Paul 117–18
Cunningham, Merce 125
Cyclonopedia 47–8, 54

Darkness 56–7, 69, 72, 73, 76, 86
Darwin, Charles 16, 98
Death 44, 50, 53–4, 58, 60, 69, 82, 95,
101, 110, 150; and Arakawa and
Gins 137; and Catherine Malabou
94; and Gao Xingjiang 93; and
Johnny Walker 74; and Killing
Commendatore 141
Deleuze, Gilles 8, 52; and desert
islands 41–3; and the fold 124,
131; and the Other 45–6, 54–7, 66;
and the wound 63, 97, 100, 103
Deleuze, Gilles and Félix
Guattari 47–8, 79; and art
141; and fascism 101–02; and
Geophilosophy 33; and money,
work and housing 35; and nomad
thought 41
Derrida, Jacques 43, 113; and carno/
phallogocentrism 109–11; and
openness 57, 59
Descartes, René 6, 148; and
anthropocentrism 14, 97; and
cogito 3, 11–12, 34; and critique
99; and dualism 117–18
Deserted island 36, 41–3, 46–8, 51,
54, 81–2, 84, 86

Digital, the 89, 136
Duras, Marguerite 94

Earth, the 3, 5, 7, 9, 18–19, 21, 23,
31, 77, 97, 101, 105, 150–1; and
another earth 26–8, 46, 47–52, 65,
75, 80, 88–9; and cracks 63; and
the earthly processes of figuring
73–4; and ecology of bad ideas 35,
37, 116; and feminism 109–11,
118; and new earth 37–40, 53–4,
57–8, 60, 82, 83–4, 87, 148; and
savageness 135–6, 138, 144–5;
and territory 33–5, 41–3, 65, 81,
84, 148; and warmer, friendlier
and more fraternal 134
Ecology 41, 53–5; and Spinoza 14
Economy 36, 50, 56, 58
Empedocles 23
Engels, Friedrich 37
Entanglement 80, 114, 135
Erasmus, Desiderius 121
Essence (Marcus Tullius Cicero and
Lucius Annaeus Seneca) 13, 37,
51, 52, 53, 97
Ethics 59, 77, 108, 112, 117–18,
122, 135; and Spinoza (Ethica:
Ordine Geometrico Demonstrata)
6–7, 99
Eudamonia 94

Feminism 8, 41, 89; and feminist
naturalism 107–15, 118
Fold/folding/enfolding/unfolding
11, 52, 59, 67–8, 86, 150; and
architecture 135; and dance
122–6, 129–31
Forsythe, William 122–5
Foucault, Michel 102, 115–17
Freud, Sigmund 70; and the three
wounds 97–100

Friday (the character) 44–5, 147–8
Friday (the novel) 43, 46, 47, 49, 79, 80, 83, 86–7

Gao, Xingjiang 93
Geometer, the 31, 33, 63, 105, 148, 151; and architecture 134, 136, 138; and dance 125–6; and economy 36; and feminism 109; and Murakami 66, 105, 150
Geometry (Spinoza) 5, 16–7, 65, 122
Geophilosophy 22, 33, 40, 48, 79, 88–9, 100, 101–02, 105, 113, 115, 118
Ghost Track 127, 129–30
Gil, José 125–6
Goat 82, 147–8; and Pan 80
Gothic, the 134–7, 145
Graham, Martha 123
Great Outside, the (the great outdoors) 11, 39, 76, 110
Groove/ungroove 31, 34, 37–42, 46–50, 53, 58–60, 101, 138, 143, 148–9
Guattari, Félix 49, 102
Guernica 145
Gunawan, Iwan 127

Haraway, Donna 100, 111–12, 114; and deconstructive critique 110; and geophilosophy 89; and situated knowledges 108–09
Haruki, Murakami 8–9, 15, 100, 105, 149; and anthropocentrism 91; and art 139–42; and the crack 63, 65; and figuring 71–4, 79–81, 150; and Hiroshige 67; and Soseki 69; and synchronicity 70; and time 95; and the wound 91
Having an Idea 3, 12, 15–18, 21, 23–8; and architecture 134; and

the Bright Idea 76; and dance 131; and geophilosophy 31, 33, 80–4; and Murakami 141, 149
Health 51, 52, 58, 60, 92–3
Hegel 36, 94, 102
Hiroshige, Ando 67
Homer 38
Hong Kong 55

Indigenous knowledges 17, 148
Intense exterior 126, 128–31
Intra-action 71, 114–16, 118, 123, 127, 133, 135

James, William 7, 98
Japan 8, 68, 74, 76–7
Javanese Gamelan 127, 130
Jung, C.G. 70

Kafka, Franz 150
Kafka on the Shore 66–7, 79, 82–3, 86–7, 149, 150
Kant, Immanuel 3, 38–40, 57
Karatani, Kōjin ix, 6, 38
Killing Commendatore 139
Kohn, Eduardo 17–18, 21
Koolhaas, Rem 136
Kundera, Milan 73
Kusama, Yayoi 101

Lake Erie 101, 116–17
Landscape 21–2, 34, 49, 67, 79, 93, 118, 141
Latour, Bruno 19, 21, 107
Laws of Nature 113–14
LeineRoebana 127
Letter to Schaller 18
Life 3, 12, 21, 26, 39, 53, 58, 60, 63, 68, 121–2, 148, 150; and feminism 109–11; and form 133–4, 137–8; and forms of life

18, 19, 22, 31, 33, 38, 83, 84, 105;
  and Murakami 70–1, 75, 77,
  85, 87, 91, 92; and a new life 42,
  46, 51, 54, 56, 59, 82–3; and the
  wound, 94–7, 99–103
Little Boy 102
Logic 75, 121; of the earth 31
Logic of Sense 45, 56
Lovecraft, H.P. 47, 65
Lucretius Carus, Titus 7, 27, 82, 121

Malabou, Catherine 94
Mannerism 136, 145
Marx, Karl 37
Massumi, Brian 17, 66, 122–3, 126
Matter 8–9, 27–8, 35, 105; and art 146;
  and between 71; and the crack 63,
  89; and feminism 108, 110–12; and
  form 105, 86–7, 122–7, 129–31,
  134–5; and geophilosophy 23;
  and God 50, 53; and imagination
  25; and materialism 16; and
  Murakami 74, 77, 84, 140–1; and
  pain 148–50; and the wound 93–4,
  97, 100
Mazakon 68
Meillassoux, Quentin 38–42, 55, 116
Menshiki, Wataru 139–40, 142
Metempsychosis 23–4
Mishama, Yukio 60
Modernism/modernity 18–19,
  23–4; and feminism 110; and
  modern architecture 134–5;
  and modern dance 122–8,
  130; and the modern museum
  143–4; and modern world
  27, 34, 43, 79, 117–18; and
  Murakami 75, 77, 79–80, 105
Money, work and housing 35–7, 42
Moreau, Francois 18
Morris, William 135
Mumming 148–9

Natsume, Soseki 69
Nature 17, 22, 23, 27, 34, 37–8, 91, 93,
  102, 110, 115, 119, 149; and art
  129, 130, 136–7; and philosophy 84
Natureculture 110–11, 114
Needham, Joseph 122
Negarestani, Reza 31, 47–52, 54–60;
  and Deleuze and Guattari's New
  Earth 57
Negri, Antonio 6, 99
Nietzsche, Friedrich 7, 39, 51–2
Nishitani, Keiji 71, 75
Nomadology ix, 6, 8, 22, 41, 50
Non-carnal birth 54, 95, 102
Nothingness 63, 71, 75, 95, 97, 140

Objects 11–12, 15, 16–17, 25, 39, 43,
  46, 63, 84, 100, 117–18, 150; and
  art 143, 146; and form 135, 137–9;
  and objects of religion, objects of
  war, objects of capitalism 144–5
Oil 27; and philosophy of oil 48–50,
  57, 151
One Flat Thing, Reproduced 124
Ornaments 76, 134–7
Otherness 11–12, 26, 28, 36, 42,
  45–6, 50, 52–7, 59, 60, 66–70,
  93, 109, 111–12, 129, 131. *See
  Anotherness, see world without
  Others, see wholly other*
other side, the 70

Paganism 148
Pain 14; and truth 147–9; and
  wounds 91–3, 100
Parsani, Hamid 47–51, 55, 57
Pascal, Blaise 19
Persevere in being 13, 18, 31, 34, 53,
  77, 88, 130
Phallogocentrism 42, 109–10
Philosophy 3, 22, 38, 42, 99. *See
  also geophilosophy, see also oil*

(*philosophy of oil*), *see philosophy of the angle;* and art 28, 84; History of Philosophy 3, 14; and materialism 8, 17, 63; and modernism 39–40, 124; and Spinoza 5, 7

Philosophy of the angle 105, 122, 124

Plath, Sylvia 143

Portrait 66, 73, 139–42

Posthumanism 8, 89, 109, 117; and Barad 114–15, 118; and Braidotti 116

present, the 3, 6, 8–9, 41, 43, 46, 68–9, 80, 83, 85–9, 121, 136, 151; and absorption 84; and the living present (Derrida) 113; and objects 143–6; and un-present 67; and the wound 95–7, 102–03

Prester John 151

Quantum mechanics 17, 71, 89, 105, 113, 115, 121

Quantum physics 114, 116, 118–19, 121

Quasi-objects 144, 148

Radical openness 55, 57, 59–60, 130

Recovery (Nishitani) 71–2

Religion 58, 130, 151; and art 144–5; and capitalism 31, 36, 43, 49, 51, 60, 82, 87; and the new earth 58

Religious, humanist and capitalist reality of the day 5–6, 9, 26–7, 35–6, 80, 84–9, 95, 97, 99, 143–4

Resemblance 82, 124, 140

Rilke, Rainer Maria 76

Robinson (Michel Tournier) and Murakami 81–7, 89; and Negarestani 44–8, 51–4, 56, 58, 60

Robinson (William Defoe) 43, 59

Ruskin, John 134, 136–7

Said, Edward 56–7, 59

Same thing, the 28, 84

Saturo, Nakata 8, 66–7, 69–77, 82–7, 89, 150

Savage 87, 133, 136; and the Gothic 144–5

Seneca, Lucius Anaeus 13, 93–4

Serres, Michel 8, 79–80, 145. *See quasi-object*; and the Garonne 15, 21–3, 28; and physics 114, 121–2, 124, 131; and reversed Platonism 140; and the wound 102

Shadows 63, 66–7, 73–4, 76–7

Sila: the Breath of the World 28

Simondon, Gilbert 7, 23–4, 66, 124

Smashing of the Amps 145

Speranza 44, 46, 48, 54, 60, 81, 83

Spinoza, Benedictus (or Baruch) 3, 5–9, 53; and *conatus* 24; and death 53; and Descartes 11–14, 99; and the geometer 122; and imagination 25, 27; and thinking 15–16, 18

Spinozist Materialism 3, 21–2, 57

Spuybroek, Lars 129, 133–8

Stockhausen, Karl-Heinz 127

Stoicism 53, 94

Subjectivity 16, 66; and feminism 109–12, 115–16; and Freud 97–8

Surface 7, 21, 26, 50, 58, 60, 65–6, 71, 80–1, 85, 89, 92, 139, 148; and the (female) body 115; and topology 124, 126, 136; and wounds 93, 95–7, 101, 142

Sympathy 13, 133–4

Sympathy of Things, The 133

Synchronicity 70, 73

Tanizaki, Junichiro 66, 74, 76

Target (become a) 53–5, 57, 129–30

Tazaki, Tsukuru 91–2, 95, 102

Tokyo 66–7, 81–2

topology 42, 52, 55, 65, 124, 126, 129; and the baker's dough 131
Tournier, Michel 31, 43–9, 51–2, 54–8, 60, 79–80, 83, 86
Tu non pensavi ch'io loico fossi? 121
Tumura, Kafka 8, 67–75, 77, 83–6, 88

Undercurrent, the (Spinozist) 3, 6–8, 16–17, 38, 48, 58, 63, 95–6, 99–100, 105, 126, 142, 148, 150, 151; and art 146; and Murakami 65–6, 72, 74, 75, 77
Unforeseen, the 8–9, 18, 75, 80, 126, 129, 134, 137
Unreal, the 67, 70–2, 79–80, 93, 105

Venus 44
Voetius, Gisbertus 99

Walker, Johnny 71, 74–5, 95, 149–50
Wallace, Alfred Russel 98
Wasp and the orchid, the 13, 17, 133
Whitehead, Alfred North 34, 117–18
Wholly other, the 22, 28, 31, 50, 56, 65–6, 82, 86, 88, 96, 113, 121, 142, 151
World without Others, the 84. *See anotherness, see wholly other*
Wound, the 22, 63, 84, 87–8, 91–103, 110, 141–2; and truth 147

Yan, Mo 147